CW00693136

WHO CARES? Dance in the Gallery & Museum

Contents

Introduction

Sara Wookey,
Independent Artist

Kate Coyne,
Siobhan Davies Dance

WHO CARES? Dance in the Gallery & Museum is a collection of 15 conversations with curators, dance artists and directors.

"Who cares?" might, at first, suggest cynicism or indifference towards the subject of dance in the gallery and museum, but rather the title emerged from the conversations with contributors, a number of whom reference care from different perspectives. The title question aims to prompt a consideration of care as it applies to dancing bodies, artworks/ objects, audiences and architectural spaces of cultural institutions that is reflective, provocative and curious.

The creation of this publication arose from our conversations and shared interests around dance when it is present in galleries and museums; which then led to the idea of gathering perspectives into a piece of print that could draw attention to any concerns without attempting to suggest solutions. Growing partly in response to the Dance Artist/Curator Mentorship Scheme at Siobhan Davies Dance, and marking the end of the pilot year, the participants of the scheme were the intended voices but as our conversations developed we extended the list to include others who had strong connections to the themes arising. All of the interviews took place between January and April 2015 and serve as a snapshot of what this diverse group of curators, dance artists and directors are thinking about at this particular moment in contemporary culture. They were asked to choose one project to speak about and were sent a series of five general questions in order to stimulate thoughts. Each meeting was approximately one hour long and was recorded, transcribed and then edited, allowing differing viewpoints to be illustrated by placing the conversations alongside each other.

This collection was only made possible by those voices who so freely and generously gave their time and insight. Any proceeds from the sale of this publication will be invested in supporting future projects which explore dance in the gallery and museum.

We hope the collected conversations prompt further inquiry into why dance in galleries and museums is being thought about and discussed at this time and to such extent, and is testament to the common desire to understand how to embrace the possibilities of dance within these spaces.

Perspectives

Andrew Bonacina

Chief Curator,
The Hepworth Wakefield

SW: Let's start by discussing your invitation for choreographers to respond to Allan Kaprow's work, *YARD 1961/2014*, at The Hepworth Wakefield.

AB: The impetus to reinvent this work by Kaprow came from a Franz West retrospective we were working on at The Hepworth. West died a year before the show opened, and suddenly several works that were designed to be physically engaged with became static due to conservation issues. For me, this provoked interesting questions around the legacy of works and practices that physically engage audiences with objects and challenge the behavioural codes of the gallery.

YARD is one of Kaprow's key early works. Shots of visitors clambering over the mounds of tyres that form the work have become iconic images of the 'Happenings' era. It was first made at the Martha Jackson Gallery in New York in 1961, where Kaprow filled the gallery courtyard with thousands of used car tyres and invited the audience to engage with them as they pleased. Kaprow was one of those figures who very early on dissolved the boundaries between art forms, bringing dance, choreography and movement into the gallery space. The idea of open-endedness was integral to the work, as he typically made a 'score' or set of instructions to allow it to be re-staged, or 're-invented' as he called it, by others. *YARD* doesn't come with instructions, only notes and images of previous iterations.

YARD at The Hepworth was the 24th reinvention of the work since 1961. But while Kaprow invited the reinvention of the work by others, for me as a curator, there were still ethical questions about doing so without the involvement of the artist. Why are we doing this? Do we have the authority to do this? It was important to me that this meta-questioning was always there, and it seemed the best way to do this was to engage a series of collaborators to pose these questions through a series of interventions. As well as the visual artists Koo Jeong-A and Rivane Neuenschwander, and musicians David Toop and Rie Nakajima, I wanted to work with dance artists as part of the project. It coincided with the moment Kate Coyne invited me to be part of the Dance Artist/Curator Mentorship Scheme and so those artists – Robbie Synge, Janine Harrington and Nicola Conibere – became involved with the project.

These artists became conversational partners in thinking through what it meant to engage with a work like this. I also left their involvement open-ended but each of them ended up realising a physical intervention into the environment. *YARD* became a frame for thinking in many ways. For these artists, negotiating both a transition into the gallery and into such a loaded physical context, it provoked many interesting questions about the codes of performance spaces. There is an assumption that when you take something out of the theatrical proscenium it relieves it from the codes that govern that space, but I would argue that the gallery is equally as coded, if not more so than the space of the theatre.

SW: That's interesting. Can you talk a little bit more about that?

AB: It becomes increasingly complex as you layer the codes of dance into a space that has its own frameworks of viewing and engagement, spaces that are even more coded in terms of the relationship between objects and bodies. There's a long history of dance and the visual arts coming together, of dance moving into the gallery space, and early on it was a very organic conversation born out of a natural exchange of ideas between visual artists, dancers, musicians, performers, etc. Very much Kaprow's era. I'm much more interested in facilitating these kinds of platforms or situations for exchange, but I often wonder whether the recent vogue for bringing dance into galleries isn't also somewhat instrumentalised by those needing to satisfy engagement agendas. This idea that it's no longer enough to present a viewer with an object, but that the museum needs to activate it in other ways, digitally, physically...

In all my conversations with those working with me on the project, but especially with the dance artists, one thing that we always wanted to be aware of was to try, as far as possible, to avoid creating any sense of hierarchy between performer and viewer. The thing Kaprow wanted more than anything with a work such as *YARD*, was to create a completely free space that allowed visitors to engage however they wished. Of course, it is still an artwork with an author, and so avoiding all hierarchy is of course wishful thinking. Anyone who steps into the space is immediately aware of becoming part of someone's work. You are immediately on display. But Kaprow was interested in physical and intellectual dynamics at play, and *YARD* becomes a perfect setting for exploring those dynamics. It became a really rich platform for the dance artists to engage with, especially as they were already thinking about how to negotiate the gallery space as a performative space.

SW: Can you speak a bit more about, as you said, 'avoiding all hierarchy'?

AB: It's impossible to erase hierarchy. The whole project was an exercise in awareness and breaking conventions. Due to health and safety reasons, visitors had to sign a waiver that made them responsible for their own safety while engaging with the installation. So that immediately signified a different mode of engagement. When there was an intervention we also had to make visitors to the space aware of what was going on. So people were made aware that either Robbie, Janine or Nicola were present, but we were careful not to call it a performance as that would potentially instate the dynamic of performer/viewer which would discourage visitors from engaging themselves. For Robbie, Janine and Nicola, that became the core of their thinking around this invitation; it wasn't about adding a temporary focus, but more about highlighting the dynamics that were already at play in the space.

SW: Just so that I'm clear, the visitors were invited to engage as well, as long as they signed the waiver?

AB: Yes, they were. And that engagement is at the heart of the work. Each of the artists dealt with the space and the conditions in very different ways. Robbie introduced additional materials into the space. He was interested in the idea of the tyre as a building tool, and so to these he also introduced boards, ropes and tarpaulins, which had a material affinity with the industrial nature of the tyre. It enabled visitors to build more proficiently, or to use the tyres in new ways. It was interesting to see how quickly audiences incorporated these materials into the structures they were already making with the tyres.

SW: In a way, re-inventing Robbie's work, too. The multiplicity of re-invention...

AB: Exactly. Robbie was very minimal in his own interventions. He would create something and you'd see people on the other side of the space starting to mimic his forms. It worked perfectly as an intervention in the sense that with such a minimal addition he was able to shape people's movement and behaviour. Janine and Nicola's interventions had a similar effect. Janine worked with another performer and introduced a series of circular mirrors that conceptually echoed the multiplicity of the tyres. They were also playing with ideas of camouflage and so often their actions were completely hidden. Nicola worked with the performer Helka Kaski, who wore a top embellished with rubber teats. Working to a minimal score, the performer's body became an extension of the physical environment. Visitors would at first stop and watch Helka perform, but very soon they were moving around her and engaging with the installation themselves.

SW: In terms of bringing the dance artists in, do the dance artists' responses and actions serve as a prompt to the visitors, to suggest, "It's OK, here are the sort of things that you can do here." Giving permission in some way?

AB: Yes, I think it did unfold like that, but it was the dance artists' sensitivity to the context and to the audience/performer dynamic that enabled them to create a sense of opportunity rather than impose a performative mode on the space. The thread that linked all of the interventions – dance, music and visual art – was the idea of liveness, being within the space at that moment.

SW: On that note, how did you deal with the crediting, naming and labelling of the dance artists' work?

AB: It was a reinvention of Kaprow's work (Kaprow always used the term reinvention rather than remake) but with the series of interventions, which were listed at the entrance to the show with their dates, clearly defined as unique to this 24th iteration of *YARD*. While the visual artists' interventions each lasted a week or two in the space, the dance artists all opted to work within the space for a single day. I think this felt more in line with their interventions being less a performance and more using the space as a testing ground or workshop.

SW: The artists are re-making the work, which is different to being in response to the artwork.

AB: It's taking the Kaprow as a situation and a prompt. There are so many threads to the project, but a lot of it came down to purely being in the space with others. The dance artists were obviously able to approach this with a consciousness of movement and being on display that a regular visitor might not have. While it's incredibly physical in terms of the tyre as an object, the work is much more environmental. The beauty of the work as a responsive space is that it can really be taken in any direction. It sounds strange to say this but even though it's an incredibly loaded space, it can also be seen as a blank canvas.
It was always the plan to sit down together and have a conversation reflecting on these outcomes of thoughts. It's still something we need to do. All three of these artists are thinking about alternative contexts, and what it means to be in other spaces of performance or display.

SW: Did you or any of the dance artists feel that it was it was enough to have the discussions and maybe not realise the live response or performance?

AB: I was completely open. There was a moment where we wondered whether it actually needed to manifest. But I think they all felt that it was a physical challenge that they all wanted to explore somehow.

SW: Is bringing in dance and performance enabling, or finding a way into a structure that feels more limiting now than years ago, when there were fewer – as you mention – codes to break?

AB: It was a complicated project to realise and it posed many challenges in terms of health and safety. But it was an incredibly popular exhibition for the gallery, perhaps because it did create this completely new mode of engagement for many of our audiences, especially audiences who might not usually visit galleries or museums. I'm not interested in curating spaces of entertainment, but someone like Kaprow was able to tap into certain elemental desires around play and interaction that perhaps allow us to think about these kinds of exhibitions with more intellectual rigour.

SW: How do you negotiate between your own personal interests, as a curator, and the expectation to fulfil certain audience needs?

AB: Everything must start with the artist and the work. I've found in the past that if you invite an artist with something specific in mind, they'll always go in a different direction but it's about being open to these about-turns. In curating live dance or performance projects in galleries you have to be open to situations that you can't predict, which can often be a challenge to the institution. The dance artists I have worked with have all been interested in engaging with the context of the gallery, and I think this Dance Artist/Curator Mentorship Scheme is born out of this growing relationship. So the projects I've worked on have tended to have a self-reflective quality to them.

In 2011 I commissioned a new project with artist-filmmaker Charles Atlas, artist Mika Tajima and her band New Humans at South London Gallery. Theirs is an ongoing collaboration that naturally brings together the visual arts, dance and music into choreographed event-based installations. For *The Pedestrians*, Mika created an installation that functioned as both an artwork and a stage set. The gallery was rigged with a dolly track and multiple cameras, and over the course of two weeks we invited various dancers, musicians, academics and artists to 'perform' in the space while Charlie filmed and live-edited the activity. For the most part it worked incredibly well, and in other ways it didn't, but that experimentation was part of the project. Some aspects were carefully choreographed, like the performances by artist John Smith, dancer Gaby Agis and a live reading by academics Nina Power and Richard Hornsey. But Charlie and Mika wanted there to be equal emphasis on the interaction and movement of visitors to the exhibition, so there were lots of impromptu or unexpected interventions. On the final day of the project, Charlie wanted to stage a 'parade' which involved us reaching out to various community groups and organisations to take part. Many were quite tentative to take part in a performance and many ended up dropping out. While a parade can be celebratory, it also carries with it political connotations which challenged people. In terms of audience participation, this kind of 'framing' proved more difficult than simply allowing them to take part through their own agency.

SW: The frame of the parade would take on different contexts and suggest different forms of agency or, even lack of agency for different community groups and organisations, is that what you are suggesting?

AB: They are framed and constructed contexts that become vehicles for physical and discursive enquiry. You're right, that questioning is always there. For me that's important because the open-ended enquiry is what makes these projects truly challenging to the institution.

SW: Does dance and performance allow you more of an experimental space of consideration than with visual artworks?

AB: I've nearly always worked with artists on a commissioning basis, so often the way in which I work is more like a producer or facilitator of ideas. When I work with dancers or choreographers in the gallery, there's always more of a negotiation because there are inevitably more challenges to be broached in working with live projects, more uncertain variables. Whether a choreographed work directly involves an audience or not, that relationship between performer and audience is still a charged one, and one that has to be carefully negotiated. For me, the process and dialogue was certainly the most interesting aspect of working with Janine, Nicola and Robbie in that situation. I don't think any of them would say that what they produced there was a work in any sense at all, or that it could be extracted from that context and presented elsewhere. It was specific to that moment and that space of thought. The project has thrown up a lot of questions for me about how we might find new ways in which to work across fields, where the structures from both visual arts and dance might be opened up and each inform the other art form.

The project with Charlie and Mika at South London Gallery was particularly interesting because of the openness of the performative space it created – where academics 'performed' on the same stage as dancers and visual artists. It was more about 'liveness' than performance really. Charles Atlas is a pivotal figure, really, both in thinking through how to create a legacy for performance through documentation, and also in working across all performative contexts, from the theatre to the gallery. Collaboration is a constant throughout all his work.

SW: Does the documentation of *The Pedestrians* work as a piece in itself?

AB: Charlie has hundreds of hours of footage from the project which will one day be edited into some kind of film, but I don't think he'd ever see it as something definitive.

SW: Where are you interested to go next with the information that you've received from these and other projects?

AB: Working in an institution means that you can introduce new strands of programme slowly over time, allowing audiences to become increasingly accustomed to new forms and thus move away from dance being something that's interruptive or interventionist. I hope to be able to increasingly work with dance artists as a core part of the programme, to the point that distinctions between a project with a so-called visual artist and a dance artist become by degrees obsolete. Visual artists are increasingly working with notions of choreography or movement, as well as mining an endless list of other fields of practice, so I do think that audiences are becoming more accustomed to approaching gallery exhibitions with fewer preconceived ideas.

These changes take time though, and it's important for me to commission new projects that have the discursive aspect we've talked about at their core. This mentorship scheme has been really valuable as it has created a forum for these conversations to take place. How can we continue these conversations and allow them to manifest in ways that will develop discourse? These conversations have always been geared towards negotiating between these two worlds, but perhaps there is a new space to be opened up that is a truly collaborative and interdisciplinary one.

***YARD 1961/2014* (2014)**
by Allan Kaprow
performance intervention by Nicola Conibere,
performer: Helka Kaski, The Calder at
The Hepworth Wakefield, Wakefield,
4 July–31 August 2014,
photo by Tom Arber,
courtesy of The Hepworth Wakefield

Florence Peake

Choreographer and Dance Artist

SW: I know that you have worked quite a lot in visual arts institutions and we have already spoken informally about your approach to working in galleries and museums. Can you talk more about that?

FP: I've worked in a few big art institutions with varying degrees of time, space, money and availability of those resources. I have sometimes had the desire to do things that were ambitious. With Yorkshire Sculpture Park it was really about that; expanding an idea which could work in one of their large galleries but also outdoors. I fundraised for that with support from Nikki Tomlinson at Artsadmin, where I am an Associate Artist, and with some support from Yorkshire Sculpture Park, mainly in terms of their in-kind resources. That was very exciting to do. And through working with other, smaller, galleries as well, I've realised that I really need to take into account what's available from the institution instead of thinking, "Big institution; big-scale bold work."

SW: And how about your work at Hayward recently?

FP: For Hayward Gallery I had a meeting with Stephanie Rosenthal where I talked about my work and then she asked me to propose something. It was very clear, after proposing, that Hayward didn't have extensive budgets or resources for this part of the *MIRRORCITY* exhibition. So I knew then that I would have to bring a previously made work, something that already exists, and adapt it to that situation. Then Frank Bock, Nicola Conibere and Martin Hargreaves got in touch with me about it, as they had been invited to curate *Volumes Project*, the performance part of *MIRRORCITY*. I knew about the little amount of resources and money, and also that it was going to be a show that involved *lots* of different artists with varying technical needs...so I was reading between the lines knowing that resources were slim: "How am I going to do something that's going to have 27 performances? And I won't be able to do all those 27 performances myself because of other commitments." But I did go into it knowing these were the conditions...so it was more about managing it.

I wanted to approach it and run the series of performances thinking of it as a practice. I thought, "Right, we are going to come and we are going to practise. We are going to practise a score. We are going to practise this piece that I did that has to do with shaking or different states of being through the act of shaking." I wanted to do a duet and I wanted it to travel through the gallery and I knew that this would mean that I would have to have a big pool of dancers. I felt very much that it is completely insulting to say, "I want to pay you to perform for, I think it was, £8.60 an hour." I didn't want to work with students; I wanted to work with professional dancers who had the experience and the maturity in understanding durational performance; understanding how to monitor themselves; understanding depth of practice and embodiment and presence in their performance. I wanted that kind of experience and my work to be represented in that way. I really wanted this idea of 'depth of practice' in the space, meaning that the performers all came to the work with a wealth of experience of practice from their own lives and artistic experience. I thought if we talked about it being 'practice' then it was the idea of getting paid to practise, like getting paid to do class or something. That we could use this space and the duration of this three-month exhibition as an experimental space. A space where, even though the score is quite tight, there can be a lot of shifts and development in that. I had 13 dancers. Most of them were from a dance background but some of them were from a theatre background. One of them was from queer performance. One of them had an unconventionally configured body.

I wanted to have the opportunity to really play with this score and see how far I could push it. What could happen? I wanted to use the exhibition/gallery space as an experiment space so that it was not just a finished piece of work that had to be performed perfectly again and again for 27 performances over three months. But how could it evolve and develop? And so, in that way, it loosened up the whole relationship to the space/hardness of the architecture and institutional context.

> **SW:** Since you mentioned the space, how have conditions been for your work in galleries and museums in terms of the qualities of the space?

FP: There is no way that there can be conditions like sprung floors. So how can we approach this harsh concrete environment? How do you look after the dancer within that score? It is a very physical score so included in it are different kinds of pacing, places of rest, stillness, and things like that. And the dancers have to take care of some of those things themselves...work with the score in a way which helps them.

What I have heard from the dancers is that it was a good experience. You know, it was part of my anxiety that they found it a rewarding experience. From the start I made a really clear proposal to the people that I invited. Stating how much, what the attitude is, what the conditions were. Then, the two rehearsals that I had were really about how we can think of this as a score, as a meditation practice. As I was really concerned about taking care of the dancers, I wanted to put a safe structure in place when they arrived and that things were being communicated clearly. There was a set of preparations as the dancers arrived at the gallery that they went through, which was some bodywork that they did with each other. We had this little warm-up space which was great.

> **SW:** How did you go about inviting artists to join this project?

FP: I wrote an email to artists I wanted to invite to perform in the work – that was titled *Swell the thickening surface of* – stating the different limits. I think a couple of people said that they couldn't work for that little money. That wasn't what they wanted. One person was angry and upset that the Hayward, this big public institution, is paying so little when they were highly skilled and experienced practitioners with 20 years' experience, or more. I think it was about reframing it in one's mind. But there is an issue of expectation...what is possible with a very tiny budget for example.

Generally I am quite flexible with conditions. I wouldn't go into lots of different spaces and expect them to start putting sprung floors in and painting the walls or doing certain things. I want to work with the conditions that are there, available to me. So if this is the money that they have, then I have a choice, and that might be to not accept the offer, even if it is from a famous institution. Across the board, there needs to be a lot of discussion about fees and money and what things are paid. That is a big issue affecting pretty much all artists everywhere.

SW: What, besides fees, do you feel is important to negotiate with the institution that you are presenting your practice in, and in regards to your need to take care of the dancers in it?

FP: Hierarchies within the institution can be difficult to negotiate, especially if you are a visitor from another art form. As performance has different needs from a static art object, it can easily be overlooked or not given quite the right conditions. In the art gallery, the performance will not always be present. It needs particular care, and how this is communicated to all front of house staff is important, as often the public ask what's going on. Crediting can be an issue; it can feel that the visual artists are placed higher than a performance artist in terms of visibility. Things like website visibility then can play an important role in how audiences know when, why, how a performance is happening in a gallery.

I feel if somebody is offering an opportunity you can always say, "No, I don't want to do it." And I felt a bit criticised by certain people at the beginning when I accepted this invitation to present at Hayward. That I should be saying, "No, fuck you," to the institution. Sticking up for dance and the whole, "We shouldn't be doing this for less money." Well, my thing is...if the dance world had more opportunities, venues, platforms and institutions supporting and presenting a range of different kinds of experimental work, there would be more choice. There aren't as many opportunities in the dance world. Part of my practice is understanding how it operates in performance with an audience, so I do want to get my work out there, to test it. I want to participate. I want to be active in the world and see how the work evolves through different interactions with different contexts and environments. So I am excited by and appreciative of the opportunities to present and test my work. I do think that it is difficult. If we all just accept low rates, and stuff like that, then that is tricky. So, it's a complex area...ethically too.

SW: What did your practice gain from the Hayward experience?

FP: I am quite interested in how the practice morphed and made the bodies merge and then the identities of the bodies shifted and changed and became a little bit ambiguous, how the form became strong. The sense of body and form in the space became very resonant. And the presence became very resonant. So, transcending the identity of the body. I hadn't understood it as much as that, and there are thirteen different dancers with different couplings. Each time the people might not know who they are going to be performing with. It was really exciting. Each time it was a shift in dynamic and energy together.

SW: In retrospect (and going back to your mentioning of fees), how did you feel about the amount of compensation that you were able to pay your dancers for the work that they did?

FP: It would have been great to be able to pay the performers more. Definitely. It was three hour blocks and, really, if you're performing for three hours that takes up most of your working day. So it did feel very underpaid.

SW: What really worked about the entirety of the project and your participation in it?

FP: *Volumes Project* was a fantastic frame and I felt very much this sense of collective, and that what we were doing was activating these in-between spaces. I felt a sense of comradeship in that, which was really good. If I was in there doing this for three months by myself I think it would have felt very lonely. So I felt there was great sense to that. The only thing is, because it was called *Volumes Project*, I felt that it slightly obscured the artists' names...six of us who presented performance works in the exhibition...I think that could have been given more publicity, as the installation artists were much more clearly represented.

> **SW:** What were things that did not work as well?

FP: There were a lot of things...where I can maybe think, "Wow, that was probably quite a difficult thing for the organisers to manage." All of these different elements. I think it was an incredibly complex project to pull off. Being listened to about needs. If it was, "This is all we've got," then I can accept that. But if they are saying, "We can do this and this and this," and then you are not listened to and things are not being met, that's when it becomes frustrating and difficult. But that could be any institution or badly run theatre, couldn't it? It's not necessarily to do with the art world.

> **SW:** What, in your experience, would you say dance – or performance – needs to have when being presented inside of a gallery or museum space?

FP: In terms of what dance needs, specifically... it depends. If you are saying, "This is all we have got to provide," that is one thing. But if the institution is wanting a very particular thing it is so different. I knew that I had to be completely self-resourceful and not rely on the institution for anything in terms of needs...technical needs or anything like that. It would have complicated things much further.

> **SW:** What benefit has there been for you in taking part in *Volumes Project* and in the context of *MIRRORCITY*?

FP: It's got to have a clear benefit. If it is not financial then there has to be some other kind of benefit. Doing the work at the Hayward has given me more visibility. It has opened up more opportunities in a wider way for me. But also I got to really test out, very explicitly, a certain practice and see how it worked. Some things you don't know what it is going to be like until you are in front of an audience or until you have the general public responding to it. I could see where the boundaries of that were and what the edges were...how bold I could be with that. That's a really exciting opportunity, but it resulted in me being only paid about fifty quid for three months' work.

***Swell the thickening surface of* (2013)**
by Florence Peake
performers: Hamish MacPherson
& Rosalie Wahlfrid,
part of *MIRRORCITY: London artists on fiction and reality*, Hayward Gallery, London,
13 October 2014–4 January 2015,
photo by Michael Brzezinski

Catherine Wood

Senior Curator, International Art (Performance), Tate Modern

SW: Shall we begin by how you came to programme Boris Charmatz's work *Musée de la danse* at Tate?

CW: I'd wanted to work with Boris for a long time since I'd met him, just before he took on the National Choreographic Centre in Rennes. When I met him – we were introduced by my former colleague Vanessa Desclaux – I was really curious about the idea of renaming the National Choreographic Centre as the Musée de la danse. Even at that point he was saying that the museum could operate more like a cabaret, it could be once a week on a Saturday. I liked the way he was rethinking the time frame of what the museum could be from the opposite perspective.

I'd written a little about his work for Artforum in 2011 but we'd first had an opportunity to present his work at the Tate at the Tanks in the opening programme in 2012. We had all kinds of ambitions for that, but it was actually quite limited in what we could do because we had one artist 'resident' per week. I'd hoped to bring a version of the exhibition called *Moments*, that they did at ZKM in Karlsruhe, to Tate, because of the way it was dealing with history and the history of female pioneers of performance. But it was too ambitious to try and transpose that here for a week, even though I thought that it was highly relevant. What we ended up doing was presenting *Flipbook*, which, in a sense, works speculatively with history as material in an equivalent way, but also delivered a dance performance that people could come to as an event. We had a kind of dual concern in the Tanks programme to make sure that we were embedding the history of performance, including dance, into the museum's base narrative of the canon of art history in the 20th century. There were, for me, museological and art historical imperatives to not make it appear like a ghettoised event space. But at the same time we wanted performances that people could come to, and that would be great. So, in that sense, and many others, *Flipbook* was fantastic!

What was interesting when Boris and his team got here was that we had scheduled in four performances which, at a certain time, you'd buy a ticket for. At the same time he was then in the space rehearsing and we said to him whether he would mind opening it up so that people could see the rehearsal process. We asked this partly because we were just opening these spaces and we thought if you arrived at a closed door it's basically closed until show time. It was, obviously, also a heavy thing to ask because they need their time to prepare. Boris said, "Well, in a way it's a bit weird if people turn up and see us warming up." I suppose warming up is about being in yourself, it's not about displaying or showing. But they went with it. They did everything in public and allowed this part of the process to be revealed.

Boris then improvised and kind of evolved part of that revelation of process into his piece *Roman Photo*, which is a visitor-participatory version of *Flipbook*. He did a fantastic thing where during part of the rehearsal he started pulling in the audience members who wanted to have a go and arranging them into the piece, somewhat spontaneously, so that they were doing it too. Luckily there were lots of Laban students who came who were willing, and that prompted other people to join in. The dancers were quite open-minded about cracking open the line between 'behind the scenes' and show time. It opened up something very interesting for us. Everything, in one way, became a performance, and at the same time everything, in another way, became process, even the actual performance itself. This open situation created a continuum that did not prioritise 'event' over 'rehearsal' or 'warm up', all somehow became equally fascinating. That was in 2012.

Through that project, a fairly small-scale invitation, we started to develop a full-scale conversation about the museum and really to try and grapple with the problem that kept being raised as a question: "Why dance in a museum?" There have been loads of conferences, talks and articles about this subject of late. Really we kept on thinking not, "What is dance in the museum?" but, "What does dance do to the museum, and how is the museum dance already?" Boris had done a really great talk at the Southbank Centre a few years before where he was talking about the whole architectural complex of the Southbank and connecting the pedestrian activity that was happening all over there – the skateboarders under the concrete and the walkways – connecting that to what's happening on the theatre stage as a kind of found choreography. He said, "If you just put on a different pair of spectacles, you would see everything is dance."

With that in mind, and by taking out the hierarchy in the Tanks piece about the performance time, ordinary rehearsal and working time and the visitors' presence, his approach somehow evens things out into being choreographic in all aspects. How does that impact on the museum? Obviously there are and have been other works in the museum and other artists that have been in our programme, like Tino Sehgal and Roman Ondák, and others who have worked with institutional critique on the question of the human infrastructure of the museum. These artists have made choreographed interventions into it in ways that highlight it as being as important as the architectural structure that we always refer to in visual art: the white cube and the wall, the plinth and all those aspects of support.

But in Boris's vision, and the way in which in Rennes he'd transposed one institutional structure into another, we really began to develop this idea: what if we imposed this label of the dancing museum on the art museum; what kind of space would that open up? Part of that is the fictional conjuring that happens just by saying it; by stating it. Like, how much is the institution shaped by the names given to it? At the same time, how would the protocols, procedures, behaviour and etiquette of a dancing museum differ from all of those associated with the care of objects, which is at the heart of our museum? So every kind of behavioural procedure here – and this is something I've worked against for a decade – is about caring for objects, protecting objects, moving objects, the lifts, the barriers, the walls, the guards – it's all about this absolute reverence where the human choreography is deferential to the object.

We wanted to think about what if we moved towards not just saying, "Here's a dance event put in the midst of that." We'd already talked a lot about that through doing the performance programme since 2002. We've already dealt with all these problems of bodies in the space, drinks in the space, whether we can use the art handling lifts to bring props, the insurance questions… all those things. But really, how could we imaginatively free the institution by pushing the idea of it being invaded by dance more radically?

SW: It is almost that the value system changes.

CW: The museum is founded within our material culture, our current value system. Dorothea von Hantelmann has written about that extensively. That's also why the anthropologist David Graeber, whom I cited in my book *Yvonne Rainer: The Mind is a Muscle*, was so important for me. The way he'd written about European traders misunderstanding the notion of the fetish in African societies as the basis of commodity fetishism. Thinking that the African traders didn't understand the value of gold because they were using it in a social ritual rather than valuing it for its inherent material properties or symbolic worth and rarity. So part of what I feel this project's doing is redistributing attention – material objects are still there, it's not about taking them out, but in pieces like *20 Dancers for the XX Century*, it's inserting other pieces of this pop-up canon in proximity to the established art canon, and unexpected relationships emerge that take away that hierarchy, I think. Because it puts the gesture on a par with the object, even if one is fleeting.

SW: Do you think this will be the first time that you test out this 'redistribution of attention'? Or has the idea been developed with each programme of dance or performances at Tate?

CW: There are other things we've done, like the first performance I organised with Mark Leckey, where he borrowed the Jacob Epstein sculpture *Jacob and the Angel* and made a sound composition for it. He said he wanted to coax something out of the sculpture, which was like an anchor in the collection to us that we all have kind of grown up with. He somehow wanted it to speak back to him. There have been all kinds of ways that, at the basic level, artists have tried to use the collection and elaborate on it through live performance. For example, Gerard Byrne did a Brechtian acting exercise for two actors and one listener, which also used the collection as a prop or a prompt. Actually, it's more visual artists who've done that than choreographers. For example, Dora García created fake tours in the collection, with a kind of guru figure who, if you listened to him, said all of these kinds of inappropriate comments about the collection works, like sexual or weird, offbeat interpretations of them, and she'd planted a group of 'followers' with him who'd listen very intently.

Andrea Fraser, as well, is in the collection. Hers is a more classic form of institutional critique, albeit in performance form. Whereas the artists I'm mentioning now are using institution in a more generative way, which I think is what Boris is doing too. It's not about deconstructing the institution. It's about how could you imagine it differently, productively. It's definitely not the first time that an artist has done that. But for other dance pieces we've done, for example Merce Cunningham, Xavier Le Roy, Michael Clark, William Forsythe, Anne Teresa de Keersmaeker, more often they have been discrete events. And then it's been the artists, like Tino Sehgal and others, who've done the more institutional interventions. So this is bringing the two things together in a much more ambitious way.

SW: It is interesting that you mention different approaches to the museum by dance and visual artists. Dancers often come from a strong physical training with less critical discourse around the art form. Perhaps visual artists are more apt to take on projects that critique the museum. Which, perhaps, is why dance artists might like being in the museum, to play more with ideas about what the art form could be. What do you think?

CW: I think, also, visual artists don't have any kind of disciplinary training now. So there's a fascination the other way, as well. Because they do have the critical mental training but they don't necessarily have the material discipline. So it's interesting...that attention – since visual art has gone towards performance so much in the past 15 years – there is a fascination coming from that...with practitioners who do come from a training on the body as a tool. From a curatorial point of view, as well, that's interesting, that level of attention to what the body can do and to staging interrelationships between people.

> **SW:** Yes, I teach *Trio A* by Yvonne Rainer more often to visual artists than to dance artists. The visual artists can be frustrated in the process of learning the dance because it is difficult. Dancers train to gain certain knowledge.

CW: As a visual artist, if you wanted to make paintings, you'd find out. As in, if you were in art school, there'd be a repertoire of materials and information you could use. All of them would be catered for in an art school, except the body, actually. You could learn to be a really good oil painter, or photographer, or edit video.

> **SW:** In returning to discussing Boris's work in Tate. Because it has not happened yet, can you share a bit about your projected thoughts about what will happen, what it will be like? Or maybe your concerns?

CW: Jack Smith said that the title is 50% of the work. I firmly believe in that and, in this case, I think it's true! It's *If Tate Modern was Musée de la danse?* Half of the project is just in that question. We're commissioning different artists and writers to write short statements that we're going to put out in advance, to generate a kind of rumour. For a lot of it we're also going to use these text-based channels, like social media and our Tate blog, to pre-document or pre-empt the project. Because it is about asking people to imagine it before they see it, just as a question. What would it be? What would a museum of dance or a dancing museum be? Especially because we're in a period of transition at Tate when the Tanks will reopen and performance, more and more, is becoming a fundamental part of what we do; because that's what artists are doing. We're pre-planting, pre-documenting the fiction of it.

On site, it will be a balance carrying that imaginative space that will be hinted at through changing the signage and the map – so tweaking the given institutional signals like the sign on top of the building, the plan and the orientation part of the volunteer guides will be replaced by the *Musée de la danse* temporarily. The Turbine Hall will have this continuous programme of choreography that's presented, changing throughout the day, beginning with the warm up that Boris is going to give that is part physical, part mental. The choreography will happen on stages in the Turbine Hall that are constructed. They will rehearse, occupy the stage, and take the stage down and build it again. We wanted this continuous sense of transformation and building because our museum is not really equipped to be the dancing museum. We don't have the right floor, we don't have the right seating, we don't have the right lights. So part of it is building it, not just to make the labour visible, but to show that it's actively in construction through time. Then upstairs in the collection galleries will be the *20 Dancers for the XX Century*, which is where the idea of the *Musée de la danse's* 'pop-up collection' occurs in the midst of our own collection displays. And in the exhibition galleries the piece called *Expo Zero*, which is the live exhibition by eight artists and thinkers will be shown.

It's that idea of constant transformation and construction. In terms of the history of institutional critique, I think that's where it differs. Even though it will draw attention to the institutional structure, it's about proposing and creating a new one, cannibalising what's here.

SW: This is something that could last a year or more. Can you talk about how you came to the decision to present *Musée de la danse* for two days versus a longer period?

CW: We couldn't afford it! The thing that makes me laugh is when people say, "You're just doing performance at the museum to up the visitor figures and bring more money in." That's so not true because it's so much more expensive. There are ninety dancers and performers in the project. It's them, their hotel and food and per diems. Human beings and in this case their specialised labour are expensive. Then some production costs and a production manager. It really is people costs and some marketing costs. But also, we liked the idea of a temporary transformation that somehow becomes permanent because it offers a new template for how things can be done.

SW: What's in it for Tate?

CW: It's hard to talk about Tate as an entity. It's just a collection of individuals. For me, I like the idea that although it's a temporary transformation, its legacy will be permanent in the memory of the institution. I've found, through doing the performance programme and also through collecting performance, that the institutional habits are so much – this is the theory of performativity in action – institutional habits rest upon precedence that people can collectively refer to and think, "When we did this, we did that. We were able to pull it off." Organisationally speaking, visitor services will think – next time they want to have naked dancing in a museum, which is a very difficult thing to achieve – "Well, we did do it then," or, "We did take water bottles in; we did manage to do the permanent building and un-building." Even though it's temporary it will change the sense of possibilities within the staff structure and the memory of the institution, which will move it. This has happened continuously through the performance programme, but also in collecting. We've had performance work that we've collected that either has no material trace, and it's a score, or it looks like an archive. It's making the first step, always, that then opens up a set of possibilities for future steps. People will think, "Well, we have that, so now we'll build on it." The institution's enactment of its own self-understanding has grown.

SW: I like the posing of the question in the title of this publication, *WHO CARES?* because we don't know how these things are done for the first time. It leaves open the possibilities for interpretation and understanding.

CW: In the arts there is a lot of focus on being relevant and of the times. To be new every time. No gallery wants to show an exhibition that another gallery has just done. I am interested in this current fascination for looking back. In particular to Yvonne Rainer's work. Why are we looking back? There is an interest in the archive, this interest to do dance in the museum again. In a way, we are reliving something that was started, maybe forgotten and then returned to. It is an interesting place to be in terms of thinking whether this moment for dance is new or not new. This moment of caring. The need to ask the question. It feels new, and at the same time a reinvention of the past. Yvonne suggested that in the 1970s the museum did not have the kind of elite status for dancers as it does now.

I think in the 70s it was really after-hours, the way dance was in the museum. Well, here, the performance things were through the education department and not the main programme. It was more like, "Well you can use the space." I know Merce Cunningham did a lot in museums. But it was never presented as a show, an exhibition, as far as I understand. Here in the history of Tate, the first performance happened in 1968 by César. It wasn't dance, but it was for private patrons of the Tate, an after-hours thing in the evening with drinks. And then there were a few things in the 70s that came in through education. It was only ever through education, associated programming, and only in the past three years have they stopped calling what I do 'Additional Programming'. I'm talking about being referred to in the organisational economy Nick Serota, Director of Tate, doesn't call it that. When Stuart Comer was starting the film programme here and I was starting the performance, we both said it should be part of the curatorial department. It shouldn't be 'in service' to the main art programme as a second tier.

> **SW:** Do you think dance has found that place in the museum? As a significant artwork among other artworks?

CW: I think we are getting there. This project we're doing now will make that proposition really clearly. The head of exhibitions here has told all the other departments, "This is the Matisse of the performance programme, so deal with it." We are getting there with the Tanks. What is great about the Tanks reopening is that everybody in the curatorial department stands and agrees that it's not about creating a space that's a kind of segregated theatre space. It will be a space where collection works and performances are shown. And equally, performance collection works will still be shown upstairs and in the Turbine Hall. The flow between the spaces is really important. As much as it's great to have a dedicated space that we can use and has acoustic treatment and has a lighting rig, at the same time we're working on sculpture shows in there that will work in tandem with showing dance.

> **SW:** There has been some speculation that future museums will start to build proper theatres with floors, showers...

CW: We have showers! And we do have a floor – though not a permanent floor because half the people don't want a floor.

> **SW:** Not all dance needs those things. It is more of a traditional need.

CW: Anne Teresa de Keersmaeker specifically didn't want a sprung floor (although I think she possibly later regretted it, because it's hard dancing on the concrete). But she wanted that aesthetic of the bare space, and it looked incredibly beautiful, how she staged her work there. In that, I do think that it's weird to cater specifically to dance, per se.

SW: Will *Musée de la danse* inform the questions about what dance does or does not need in the museum?

CW: Yes, our production manager Judith Bowdler, who is very involved in this, and Steve Wald, who's a freelance production manager we have worked with for over a decade – are very much a part of an active conversation. I wouldn't say just for this project though, because everything we've done in the past twelve years has been building towards that awareness, for me, to feed into what's in the Tanks and what isn't. Although it's easier to use the South Tank because it's acoustically treated, visually it's a slight shame that they had to spray it with that black acoustic material. So it's kind of a question of what do we need to essentially put in and what do we need to keep out in order to keep it raw and beautiful as a space.

SW: It is interesting, as a dance artist, to think about how the relationship between the space and body might have an effect on the kind of work the dance artist makes. In one way, the fact there are different kinds of spaces in a museum gives the opportunity for the choreographer to think about different kinds of work or ways of working to adjust or adapt to the space. Whereas if we just move to a traditional theatre we are assuming that choreographers want to make work that fits into that kind of space.

CW: In the round gives such a different sense of the work for the audience – I was thinking of Black Mountain College which had the audience arranged around the work – which is essential to me for how we use the South Tank, as well, which has a natural centre and four sections. Where you're aware of yourselves as an audience body, which for the way visual artists work is usually so important. Anne Teresa also worked with that as a choreographer when she was here.

SW: Would *Musée de la danse* happen – as it will here – if every museum had perfectly equipped theatres?

CW: No, the question wouldn't be so vital for them, how to inhabit our space. And we would probably feel, "Well, we've kind of dealt with them because we've got the space for dance." It probably wouldn't bleed into the infrastructure in the way that I'm saying it does when you have a dancer performing on the floor of the Turbine Hall in proximity to a standing visitor, in proximity to a museum attendant. You start to see this continuity of bodies with different functions.

I think it was significant for us that we were proposing this proposition at this point in the history of Tate, in the evolution of Tate. Before the opening, not after it. Because we're still in the state of being a bit unfixed. I feel the ambition and reach of this fiction should have more purchase on when we – it almost explodes the possibilities for the Tanks to reappear as a container for performance. Because it's already shown it can't be contained like that and it affects the whole being of the museum set up, which is performative. It's interesting how much people inside the museum, in all departments, have come on board with the idea. I was thinking that if I'd said to them, "We're doing a post-institutional critique performative iteration of how the museum could behave differently," they'd be asleep before I'd got through. But if you say, "We're creating the dancing museum," it's quite fun on one level and then people have got into the complexity from there. Because dance is at the heart of it.

> **SW:** And even dance as an adjective: the 'dancing' museum.

CW: I never got to the bottom of this with Boris. Why they choose to use 'Dancing Museum' in English and '*Musée de la danse*' in French. It's quite different. That's how they use it there, and we took it from them.

> **SW:** In considering the dancing museum at the scale that it will be presented at Tate – and I think there is also a disco ball? – I am curious where the slippage is between dance as a fine art practice and the spectacle that it can become. Can you reflect on that?

CW: I've always been interested in spectacle. Some of the first stuff we did here – Carlos Amorales, a Mexican wrestling match, which turned the Turbine Hall into a massive sports arena with people cheering, that was one of the first things I did. I think spectacle is a glue that makes the audience aware of themselves as a body of people; something that you don't usually get in a museum because everyone's usually atomised and individualised and on their own trajectory, and the museum's set up to be that. I think it's quite interesting when you have occasional moments, which is what Carlos did quite deliberately and what this will do to some extent, that crystallise the mass of people wandering around Tate into watching something together, and then disperse again. I really like the fact that the museum offers a space where that can happen, where the formation isn't predetermined like in a theatre. What would be one of things I want to commission is a set of photographs of this piece, of the audience configurations that will happen throughout this project. There will be so many of them, as each set is constructed or deconstructed, or as the audience is learning – Boris wants to teach bits of the dance as a kind of giving away the heritage for free. I would like to do a time lapse film document of how the space changes over the two days.

We're having an ethnographer come and do a study of Tate before *Musée de la danse*, and on the weekend as well, because that's part of our documentation of the project. He will do this ethnographic study of people's behaviour on a normal day.

It has been very much a collaboration. Boris specifically wanted it to be this way, because he didn't just come here and say, "I want you to name this the *Musée de la danse*." Sounds somewhat colonial! We invited him to come and test his proposition. He's bringing the dancing, the dance and also the concept – it's his work that is at the heart of it and inspired the whole concept. But, at the same time, my interest as a curator here obviously is partly what it does to the art, but also what it does anthropologically to the structure of the museum. And there are these pressure points in terms of care, between the classic one – whether the dancers can bring water in, which they need – and collection care – being worried about the artworks on display – but also pressure points around audience behaviour, for example, Yvonne Rainer's *Chair Pillow* dance...the audience will want to start joining in and the unpredictability of the audience behaviour in that situation. Collection care wants to take certain works out, and put new barriers in. Negotiating all that...we don't want anyone's hand through the artworks...it's our duty of care through government insurance and the indemnity of Tate's collection that we can't be irresponsible.

SW: And the care for the audience, the participants.

CW: That's true. We can't just have people performing *Chair Pillow*, because they aren't allowed to stand on a chair.

SW: Or throw pillows.

CW: I think they are allowed to throw pillows. But not stand on chairs because that's 'working at height', and opens up a whole other health and safety conversation...!

***If Tate Modern was Musée de la danse?* (2015) by Boris Charmatz**
performers: Boris Charmatz & Peggy Grelat, Tate Modern, London, 15 & 16 May 2015, photo by Hugo Glendinning

Nicola Conibere

Choreographer

SW: After my prompt to choose one project to speak about, I am curious which one you had in mind?

NC: I am inclined to speak about *Volumes Project* at Hayward Gallery, probably because it was most recent. It was a project that began with a much closer relationship with a curator than other gallery works I have done. It's relevant to say that I have shown work in galleries before but always through dance organisations or as part of a dance festival. Most notably, I've shown work at Nottingham Contemporary, where I have presented a few works, always through Dance4. It was striking for me that the first time I showed a work there – which was a three hour piece – I think the chief curator of the gallery came for the last ten minutes. He caught the end of it. As far as I know, for all of the projects that I have shown since at Nottingham Contemporary, nobody from the curatorial team at the gallery has seen them. I think the gallery's relationship with Dance4, as I understand it, is that they trust them as an organisation and want dance to have some kind of presence in the building. So they outsource to Dance4 and of course Dance4 are then able to work with this beautiful venue.

SW: Can you speak about the relationship that you had with Hayward for *Volumes Project*?

NC: The relationship with Hayward, from the start, was very different. I received an email one day from Stephanie Rosenthal's assistant saying Stephanie wanted to meet with me and talk about my work. So from the beginning that was about sitting down with her and having a conversation about my practice. We spoke in some depth about my work. She had been on my website, looked at clips of different pieces, and had questions. There was a level of engagement with my practice that was not afraid to incorporate aspects of philosophy and conceptual ideas which are important to my work and that I sometimes feel that I have needed to hide more in some dance contexts. There is a fear of sounding overly academic or that such ideas might alienate audiences. But this felt like a rare opportunity to go with what is in the work and with what contextual questions might come up. The prospect of showing something at Hayward and working with Stephanie was immediately appealing because here was someone who was engaging with my work. What was also satisfying about that conversation was Stephanie's frankness about being very interested in contemporary dance practice and her feeling, perhaps, that she doesn't get to see as much as she'd like. She was basically saying that she is aware there is a lot of interesting work happening in London at the moment, the focus of the exhibition being London, which is why that was relevant and she was keen to discover current practices and explorations she might not be aware of.

What the conversation turned into was me talking about other practitioners who I thought were interesting. Not just practitioners, but other people involved in the independent dance world in London, and other people setting up spaces, different projects...and she wanted to hear different perspectives on that. I appreciate the space she created for that and it wasn't instructive on her part – far from it. And then the possibility of me working with Frank Bock and Martin Hargreaves quite naturally grew to articulate the part of the exhibition that would feature contemporary dance and choreographic exploration.

Stephanie is also a very practical thinker, and this exhibition she was organising, called *MIRRORCITY*, had to be turned around very quickly. So, there was something practical about outsourcing to us; in a way we were trying to avoid the word 'curator', but to take on a sub-curatorial role when it came to the dance artists.

SW: Can you talk more about this role and what excited you?

NC: I was excited at the proposal of Martin and Frank. These were people who she knew, and I know them both but had not collaborated in this way with them before. Mostly I thought it would be an opportunity to work with them in a more creative capacity, with the idea of creating a framework through which to host choreographic practice in a visual arts context. If Stephanie had asked whether I wanted to organise this myself, I think I would have resisted because I would have felt that I don't have the authority to do that, and couldn't have done it alone in that timeframe. The prospect of collaboration was very interesting to me, and it was quite specific to those conditions, quite specific to those people.

SW: What was most valuable to you about the project?

NC: I would say the level of trust that Stephanie gave us in conceiving *Volumes Project*...in conceiving a group of artists and collection of practices that would speak to each other. Not just conceiving a group of artists but before that, in conceiving *how* dance might be present in an exhibition. She responded to our suggestion that we don't have a dedicated room because we wanted to avoid anything like a stage. Likewise our suggestion that we would not have performance times. These ideas were offered with the hope that the choreographic work might sit with greater equality amongst other objects or other media that were present in the exhibition space, and not be separated by a sense of special event that timed performances or a stage might provoke. We were given space to conceive how dance might participate in this exhibition, and Stephanie supported our suggestions.

SW: Practically speaking, how did you, Frank and Martin work together, as you said, as co-curators and in collaboration with Stephanie, who curated *MIRRORCITY*?

NC: The three of us decided we would like to do it, and in terms of conceiving the project, Martin and Frank and I regularly met and talked. We continued to meet with Stephanie in that time. The focus of those conversations with Stephanie was necessarily predominately practical. Things like determining that we needed to do an Arts Council England application, and covering contributions; the gallery could feed into that. Of course, we were sharing our ideas about the artists we wanted to invite and why. As I recall, at no stage did Stephanie question or obstruct any artist we were suggesting, or what work they might be doing, but she was very happy to enter conversation about the nature of their work. In addition to acknowledging the trust that Stephanie gave to us, after the exhibition had finished we met to reflect on the project. She said something that she had said once before, and it's valuable to hear. She said that she would have made different choices, and she thinks they might have created a less interesting contribution to the exhibition than the ones that we made. And that this was a direct result of us being immersed in that world, and in touch with practitioners and what they're exploring. She spoke about how she might have veered more towards works that expose process a bit more, or more explicitly. She made a suggestion that some of the works that we invited brought with them questions about sculpture, for example, which she hadn't necessarily anticipated on being present...so some of the works that had a more solid presence or moved slowly, or something like this. Of course, it is gratifying for us to hear that...it's interesting to hear that perspective from her. That she hadn't had access to this work, maybe wouldn't have conceived of this project in quite the same way. Which was the whole point of inviting us to do so.

SW: Was there anything about the project that, in hindsight, you would have done differently or wished was different?

NC: It was a very challenging project. I am conscious that I am speaking very positively about it because there were a great many positive things. I think we created something very interesting; a choreographic project in a mixed-media exhibition, where the live work is present alongside the other media without hierarchy, without being differentiated by timed events.

One of the points of possible difficulty I interpret as a point of huge artistic interest is the issue of signage, our names and the names of our works. I can speak, in particular, in relationship to the piece that I showed, which was called *Do-Re-Me*. It involves two performers wearing heaps of black fabric, who are wrapped around each other and they roll through the gallery, sometimes very slowly, and sometimes they pause. We usually presented it upstairs at Hayward, and the signage for *Volumes Project* was downstairs. On many occasions, when I was watching, there were people looking for a sign on the wall asking, "Who is the artist?" or, "Which artwork is this?" So there was this question around our works and our presence as artists. Our role as artists of those works was less present than the names of the visual artists whose names were on a sign next to the work that did not move. Could we do anything about that? There were lots of conversations around this. Initially I started seeing things happen with my work that sincerely interested me. I started taking a series of photos of it. Because it moved – and moved slowly – the work would keep on rolling underneath the sign for another artist's work and might pause there. And then I would see somebody visiting the gallery. I'd see a visitor look at the performers and instinctively start reading the sign that was next to them, clearly associating what was on the sign with the performers, even if they had just seen them roll there. I thought this was wonderful so far as the project was interested in exploring the reaches of the choreographic within a typical visual arts scenario, within an art exhibition. So I now have a series of photos of this piece next to signs for different artists and artworks. It's like it's trying out different authors and different descriptions of itself.

This is just one way in which the work is subtly disrupting, and therefore revealing, the nature of the conventions at work when we look at art in galleries; simply by rolling along next to a sign, in full view, and then still having people making an association between the artist's name on the wall and the work. I quite enjoyed, then, watching this piece roll through the gallery and, essentially, collect authors, different titles and explanations for itself. Sometimes visitors very quickly realised it wasn't connected to the sign it was next to, and other times there remained this uncertainty as to whether there was a connection or not. Certainly, so far as revealing how conditioned we are to stand in front of the object, look at the sign on the left and look back at the artwork, I thought it was a lovely, subtle way of unsettling that kind of convention or revealing that convention.

SW: It sounds like the potential 'problem' was very generative to your thinking about your practice. In terms of the issue of signage, how did you negotiate titles for yourself and crediting for the curatorial work you were doing while also being an artist in the exhibition?

NC: I know I used this term 'sub-curator'. It is an inaccurate term, because there was an entire exhibition there. Stephanie conceived and curated that exhibition. And she curated us as part of it. In a way we were like a collective. There were other artists in the exhibition who are collectives; LuckyPDF, Lloyd Corporation and Pil and Galia Kollectiv are all made up of several artists. I remember the point at which we were deciding how to deal with this. Something I am also very wary of is crediting people in such a way that actually throws tons of information at a public who don't understand the nature of those relationships and end up bombarded with words and names. So it felt interesting to propose a kind of temporary collective, but also useful to simplify the message. This decision to call ourselves *Volumes Project,* and to include the artists' names and our names, felt important in terms of – not accessibility – but making the information easier to handle.

The other thing to say, in terms of curating, is: it's only people who had regular access to the exhibition, and the exhibition as a whole, who understood *Volumes Project* as curating six artworks. Most members of the public would visit the exhibition once and encounter one of those pieces, so what they would experience wouldn't be our curatorial decisions; what they would experience was one part of it, whereas they did experience Stephanie's curatorial choices.

SW: How was scheduling decided upon and what was the level of concern for the visitor to the gallery, who might be looking to see several dance works in the spaces?

NC: We managed to do six hours a day, but the gallery was often open several hours longer than this, so there were always one or two hours without a work from *Volumes Project*. Also, performers took breaks, so our presence wasn't constant. But we had a physical presence for most of the hours the gallery was open.

Going back to the question of credit; we had these conversations with Stephanie that if we call ourselves *Volumes Project*, we have no identity. We have no identity online, no presence. If people read about us on a press release from Hayward, or if visitors see the work and look us up, there is no website. There was already a problem, which was that in the exhibition the availability of our names as artists was less than that of other artists showing, because of the nature of our work moving while the signs stayed still. Also, if anyone wanted to look us up, we didn't have a website. We had a page on the gallery website. But that was slow to appear. That's one example...we were clear about our concern about that early on. We were going to take on the name *Volumes Project* and offer ourselves as a temporary collective, but if people want to find out about our work then they have nowhere to go. In terms of presence and credit, that was a more negative point.

This is also where we felt a responsibility to these artists in *Volumes Project*, and this is where other conditions came in. The artists weren't getting paid very much. Being aware of this wider economy in which artists work for free for high profile venues, and of course this was a high profile venue, it has to be worth it for what you get back from it. Dealing with the situation where we have a low profile. So, already, we have an issue of being an ethereal presence.

SW: What you may be pointing to is that there is a need to market work and to be visible in an art market.

NC: The reality of being in an art market...yes, it takes me back to the comment about my work and the signs. Professionally, this is probably not very good for me at all, because a lot of people seemed to be loving this work but they have no idea who it is by. But as an artist, I was thinking, "This is very interesting; what it is doing in the space; what it is revealing about this place." It is a shame no one knows who it's by. But it's that dilemma. It is the difference between the work art does, as in the work of the artwork, and being a worker as an artist. And having to deal with the market and certain aspects of presenting yourself as a professional and things like this.

SW: How did you and your colleagues decide on the title *Volumes Project*?

NC: The decision about what to call the project was one of those Skype conversations that wasn't allowed to end until we made a decision about what to call ourselves. If one of the basic things at work in the project is this question of the reach of the choreographic in a visual arts exhibition, we focused on what new experiences of bodied encounter it might bring: experiences of bodies creating space, rather than moving in-between; bodies creating new experiences of space and new experiences of material relation. It was understanding body as material, but materials that generate relations.

Those relations are often experienced as space, maybe a density of space. We were looking for a term that would really encapsulate these aspects of these concerns. So 'volumes' felt a very useful term. You have the physical volume of the body, but also, the reaches of – I am trying to avoid overly dancerly terms here – but the potentials of the expansion of space, and its role in affecting how we relate to other material, as well. 'Volumes' as referring to experiences of density or different qualities of densities in a space or in a place. It seemed to have that all covered, basically. Of course, there is that implication of noise, as well. The implication of volume up and down, the immediate implication of scale. The works within *Volumes Project* existed on different points on a scale of experiences of volume.

***Do-Re-Me* (2014)**
by Nicola Conibere
performers: Neil Callaghan & Ben McEwen,
part of *MIRRORCITY: London artists on*
fiction and reality, Hayward Gallery, London,
13 October 2014–4 January 2015,
photo by Michael Brzezinski

Robbie Synge

Choreographer and Dance Artist

SW: How did you begin showing your work in gallery or museum spaces?

RS: I'm quite a newcomer to dance, at least professionally. My background was in science and physiology. I studied in Edinburgh, and I worked in the health and the education sectors in the UK and abroad. I got into dance the long way around. I certainly haven't made work specifically for museums and gallery spaces up to now. It's not been a driving interest or mission of mine. I was interested in the boundaries – in what I see as quite fairly rigid boundaries – in the dance sector. For me, a sense of boundaries in dance started, at least, in training in an institution. I trained at Laban through a one-year programme. I was in my late twenties at the time, so I didn't really want to be in an institution again, in education. I wanted to get on with learning by doing, building on my existing professional experiences. Going into this institution I did find that I had a yearning to connect to makers and artists working outside. I enjoyed the perspective that it was giving me, but I felt like there was something missing there. So I felt like, perhaps in dance, it might generally be more institutionalised, more of a kind of bubble than perhaps general art school, where at least you'd have animators, visual artists, filmmakers and so on around. I sense that visual arts have been a more open environment in this way. That's the root of my sense of boundaries in dance, maybe: in education.

Looking at history, I see that dance in museums and galleries happens in waves. It seems to be a striking thing at one point in time, and then we come back to it later. And yet, maybe, there is another drive as to why it should be happening, and why isn't it just a permeable boundary?

SW: Can you talk about how you came to be a part of the Dance Artist/ Curator Mentorship Scheme?

RS: I got into Dance Artist/Curator Mentorship Scheme from seeing the callout online from Siobhan Davies Dance, and that this would be a pilot year of the scheme for three dance artists/choreographers and three curators. I did a written application, and then a Skype interview, in my case, because I am based relatively remotely in the Highlands. I liked that this dialogue was quite open. That it was about gauging inspirations and ideas and aims. I was just interested, really, in lines of inquiry, and I addressed a few of those in the scheme application. Then meeting the curator for the first time, Nicola Lees, Curator of Frieze Projects London, I didn't really have a set agenda or things I wanted to address in our first meeting, or, particularly, a set agenda of what I wanted to achieve in the year, to be honest. I feel more curious about having these conversations than actually trying to make things happen. Speaking to Kate Coyne, who designed the scheme...she reminded me that so much comes down to a conversation between two people and that talking can lead to all sorts of things. I suppose I got the sense immediately with Nicola, who has worked in many well-known art institutions and art galleries...that she had wide networks and awareness of the visual arts but, perhaps, not so much in dance. So, again, I am quite early career but I think I was able at least to offer my perspective on that and test the waters to a certain extent.

SW: Tell me about one particular work that you have done in a gallery or museum context.

RS: I was wondering whether I could even start to talk about this one project that I did at The Hepworth Wakefield, which came out of the Dance Artist/

Curator Mentorship Scheme and was an opportunity that arose on very short notice. I feel like everything is quite intertwined; the scheme and the experience at The Hepworth itself. They are really related for me.

It was very soon after that first meeting with Nicola, or around that time, that this opportunity with one of the other curators, Andrew Bonacina, at The Hepworth Wakefield arose, where he was showing a Franz West exhibition. He wanted, alongside that to bring in *YARD 1961/2014* by Allan Kaprow. This work is one of Kaprow's environment works, which is a huge space full of rubber tyres. Kaprow called it an 'environment', rather than a 'happening'. Andrew invited the three dance artists – Nicola Conibere, Janine Harrington and me – on the Dance Artist/Curator Mentorship Scheme to engage in this environment; to respond to it, and to reinvent it in some small way. The three of us were also in the company of a few visual artists who were asked to do a similar thing. The three choreographers would have a chance to really get involved in something. For me, that was my first significant interaction with a gallery space in a choreographic way. I would never have got to do that, otherwise, had it not been for this scheme. I feel that I am learning a lot very quickly.

> **SW:** What was the process like at The Hepworth Wakefield – did you do any preparatory research? And did you have any relationship with the gallery and that particular work of Kaprow's before accepting the commission?

RS: It all came about very quickly, so timescale was definitely on my mind immediately. So it's not something I set out to try and achieve; it's not an idea that I had in mind. It was just an opportunity that arose, and I was trying to think about it very practically, and could I make the most of this within my current practice and almost use it as research. I think it worked to a certain extent and, in other ways, perhaps it isn't something that I have referred back to much. I have been working a lot with objects and, in a practical way, reinterpreting their utility and function. Something I have appreciated more recently is really linked to my interests growing up – my interests in technique, physical technique, martial arts and skateboarding. Interacting with an environment often through use of another object or static thing. It was relatively early stages of that research, and I decided I had no connection, really, with Wakefield, with this building and, not particularly, with Kaprow. It was a bit of an art history learning for me. I decided I would introduce a few tools into the space that people might be encouraged, through seeing me engaging with them, to join in. Simple things like bits of 2x4 wood and a big sheet of tarpaulin, a rope, some flat boards and platforms. People would be encouraged to engage with the tyres, because it's, more or less, a wall-to-wall sea of tyres. It's a sort of a dynamic sculpture and environment where people move the tyres around and build towers, create pathways or forts, or whatever. It's quite dynamic in that way. I mean people are on top of these tyres and stumbling around and that creates risk. It was apparent when I was there and talking to Andrew, his desire to not compromise on Kaprow's instructions and to not compromise based on the health and safety issues of various others, perhaps, in the space, in the gallery. For me, that was in the back of my mind when I was considering it, but I was encouraged by him to do what I wanted to do.

> **SW:** How did your work engage, or not, the gallery visitors?

RS: I had these tools that people could interact with on top of or amongst the tyres. I was always aware of the physical danger and I had no idea if people would want to get involved with what I was doing, or if they would want to stand and watch me. My motivation was that I wasn't going to be performing for them. I was going to be in the space, perhaps giving permission or encouraging permission to be involved in something. Thinking about a gallery space with people moving around and not sitting in seats watching and asking, "Why do this in a gallery and not on stage?" That worked to a certain extent. It was very playful, very exploratory. There were lots of children around. It was nice to observe and watch, for them to observe me. It had a long, slow, relaxed feel to it. There was quite a lot of interaction with the invigilators. It was very open. I think I liked it because there was a lack of intensity. It was quite informal. It was quite playful. Yet these tyres being so striking, and all of the meaning that can convey: the environmental concerns, the dead objects... the darkness...the dirt. Yet build some platforms and speak to each other and collaborate...something functional. It was a great opportunity to have met and have engaged with that kind of an institution and given that permission.

People encountering the artwork, when I was there, were from all different backgrounds, and I can only assume that certain people had certain information of who I was and what the idea was. This space, full of these tyres, in and of itself is overwhelming. You kind of disappear in there a bit. It's a kind of twitch within this big space that's something else. It's a detail, maybe, to pull you in. But it might not pull you in. I think there were notes, quite small, but there was a lot of information. I really appreciated how they had done it. There was an end wall on the other side that had a nice documentation of the history of *YARD*; different incarnations in different spaces, and photos. There was a small amount of information with, I think, different dates, different artists. Not particularly prominent, but there to be found.

> **SW:** How do you feel about dance being presented in gallery and/or museum contexts?

RS: I don't have huge amounts to say about dance in galleries or museums, specifically, but I can talk about how I feel about it, what I sense the differences and challenges are. I think, from what I have seen and heard recently and, occasionally, viewed in the past, that it is often...in terms of what artists need... the process of making...the values. They can often be very different, but also in terms of the art itself and...that comes down to both artist and curator...about what is going to work in the space or why bring a dance work into a gallery space and not elsewhere?

> **SW:** How did you and Andrew negotiate and did your value systems align in terms of how to present your work, and in relation to Kaprow's work, in the gallery space?

RS: Andrew and I agreed that it was valuable to present my work in The Hepworth, in that it was a brief interaction. It was a day and a half. And I think the other two choreographers had two similar short spells. Which is fine, logistically and that was the way it needed to be for me. So we agreed that it had worked well within that time span. But I think we also talked quite a lot about politics and the openness and how to make things happen. How to open up to each other in some way, and perhaps it's to do with cultures within each sector...if you call it two different sectors...or the gallery/museum world and the dance world. I think we talked a little bit about how we worked and what we felt was important.

We talked about values, and thinking about dance in terms of time and space, and space being important, and site-specific work. After all, the gallery or museum is just another space. We make site-specific work for the river out there or near the railway station or whatever. It's just about how we can really respond to gallery spaces, from my point of view at least, in an interesting way that's not necessarily about bringing in some piece of repertoire or some project and flying it in and putting it in yet another gallery white space. I can't sense a huge difference between doing that and touring theatre, different black boxes. And I suppose we connected in thinking about this environment piece and the logistics of how that would work.

There was also a useful crossover from my experience at The Hepworth Wakefield with *YARD 1961/2014* to this new piece of mine, where I want to really try and spend time in the theatre beforehand and to adapt to the features of the space and try and bring that to life in some way. It happened very quickly, so I kind of logged that experience and got on with another work, which is a staged piece. In some ways, I think the most successful aspect of it was being able to have conversations with Andrew there; to have maintained that connection with him and for him to have pointed me in certain directions.

SW: It sounds like you are interested in dance being in response to the site of the gallery or museum and, also, the theatre?

RS: Of course there are works out there that have been made in galleries that don't have that response to the space as a concern necessarily. I think it's interesting when you start to consider an existing piece of work and bringing it into a gallery space...what are the considerations around that which are important: where people stand, or light, or viewpoints... It's all a design in some way. And there are often choices that we make as choreographers or makers, and there are choices that curators can be aware of.

SW: How did you approach *YARD 1961/2014* and how did that feel?

RS: Approaching this environment is overwhelming. It's the scale of it, the intensity of it in some ways. It's just there. There is no denying it. It's not taking it and doing something with it. It's an invitation to respond and to add in some way. Or to activate or suggest that it could it be something other. I felt really excited about it, obviously, and quite terrified. Just the name, the scale, being in that space and being associated with The Hepworth Wakefield even very fleetingly, for me, was a big deal. Artistically, I felt like I needed to be true to my own interests and to suggest something that could happen. Not try too hard to state what this is. Try not to be too bold, in a way. I was, again, inviting something of people, really, rather than messing or meddling with it too much.

SW: I am wondering, from how you are speaking about your approach, if you categorise your work as dance or, perhaps, as something else?

RS: I can talk about understandings and awareness. I guess people can have things in their mind. Everyone has their ideas about what dance is, or can be. We're all learning all of the time. I suppose there is a certain amount of presenting possibilities, openings to ideas about what this might be. For me, if I am going to put something in a gallery, I would like it to not be a sort of acute audience encounter, watch-and-leave type of thing. I feel like something that suits my approach generally in movement, and what interests and excites me, is of a lesser intensity, perhaps. It's more something that can be observed, dipped in and out of, and is responsive to the space and allows engagement on different levels. By that I mean you can sit with it and find more in it for a while, or you could chance upon something briefly and move on. It's not going to be something that is parachuted in and put in the corner where everyone can see.

***YARD 1961/2014* (2014)**
by Allan Kaprow
performance intervention
by Robbie Synge, performer:
Robbie Synge, The Calder at
The Hepworth Wakefield, Wakefield,
4 July–31 August 2014,
photo by Tom Arber,
courtesy of The Hepworth Wakefield

Yvonne Rainer

Choreographer and Filmmaker

SW: As a way to get started, could you speak about a recent dance work in a gallery or museum?

YR: One of Boris Charmatz's dances at the Museum of Modern Art titled *Musée de la danse* was about dance all over the museum with people coming and going. Constant distraction. Very difficult sound-wise if the performer was talking. The performers were asked to introduce what they were doing. I was there and you couldn't hear what they were saying because of the lousy acoustics, because of the constant buzz of the visitors to the museum. Some choreographers adapt and use this kind of ambience, but others want a concentrated situation with the audience in one place and in comfortable seats. Being the old fashioned choreographer that I am, I'd prefer the latter. So the museum is not an ideal place for me. I have had the experience of *Trio A* with a curator wanting the audience to walk through it! *Trio A* is frontal. It has this very specific relation to the audience. These are art historians who don't know their dance history. They don't really know what they are getting into or what they are looking at. That, probably, is changing now. Everyone is asking these questions about what is required in the museum, who is adapting to what and to whom? Those are basic questions. My question initially is, "Why are the museums interested in dance now?"

SW: What do you think dance demands from the museum?

YR: I would like the museum to have different kinds of spaces for dance. Classical black box with retractable bleachers, a lighting grid, a sprung floor. That is another thing, the concrete floors are hell. The dancers are not protesting this. I have an ageing group and they are asking for an injury if they have to dance without a sprung floor. Also dressing rooms and showers and a living wage, or more in remuneration comparable to art world norms. Which brings up the idea of the collection. How do museums collect dance? Obviously, by documentation which they should purchase.

SW: Have you ever been approached by museums which want to purchase your work?

YR: No, that is another thing. In June I will be presenting a new work at MoMA. They will make a documentation that might be sold. I will still have the rights. My dancers will be paid what they are usually paid, for tech time and for warm up time and for the performance itself.

SW: Is MoMA recording the performance and do they own that as a document?

YR: They will own the video documentation. I guess they can show it whenever they want. Now that is a question: should the choreographer get royalties every time the documentation is shown in the museum? MoMA owns prints of several of my films. They show them and I don't get anything from that. They own them, they bought the prints. I don't know... I guess it's unreasonable to demand that the rights of the documentation should include royalties whenever it is shown. After all, visual artists aren't compensated when their work in a museum collection is shown in the same institution.

SW: Has anyone has ever approached you to purchase the film documentation of *Trio A*?

YR: Sure, I have a distributor, Video Data Bank, which either rents or sells DVD copies.

SW: Has anyone wanted to purchase the live performance of *Trio A*?

YR: How? Well, that is the thing; I think Tino Sehgal is the only person who has sold a live piece of choreography. It's a very questionable deal. He demands no documentation, no record, just a handshake! I don't know how he gets away with it!

SW: Do you think museums are getting more used to paying artists for the labour of making the work? For example, paying for rehearsals?

YR: Well...yes, if they commission a work. I will get a fee from MoMA.

SW: Do you mind me asking how much you pay your dancers?

YR: My dancers get paid $25 per hour for rehearsal and $800 per performance, whatever the length; for an evening of dance.

SW: How were the conditions at Raven Row in terms of fees, paying dancers, etc.?

YR: We can both talk about that because you were a part of it. That was a seminal experience. Twelve people in two casts doing four shows a day for a month and being paid adequately, yes?

SW: It could have been more...

YR: What were you paid?

SW: I recall being paid £11 per hour for rehearsals and £12 per hour for performances.

YR: Not nearly what I pay my dancers.

I had a similar conversation with Catherine Wood. Say they present a visual artist's work. That work stays up for two months and draws in a daily audience. What was unusual about *Yvonne Rainer: Dance Works* at Raven Row was that my dance work was performed four times a day for a month. Whereas, usually, a performance takes place for only a few nights, at most. And then the audience is gone. At Raven Row, although there were only thirty people at each show because of the limited space, the month-long duration ensured that a sizeable number of people saw it.

SW: Did you feel that your documentation, notes and sketches alongside the live performance works at Raven Row were felt as either two separate things or that they informed each other?

YR: Yes, I think they informed each other. For instance, the notebook entries, photos, and graphics that were on display made it possible to see the origins of the dances. It was a good situation. There were, also, different kinds of audience relationships. You could take your time through the exhibition and then go sit for an hour in the performance.

SW: Some people that I have spoken with have talked about being in the theatre in contrast to being in the gallery or museum. And some of the dance artists are saying that they don't make a conscious decision to perform outside of a theatre, it is just that the theatre is not inviting them in to show their work, whereas the galleries are. Which brings me to the fact that *Trio A* was not made for a theatre space...

YR: *Trio A* was made for the Judson Church space, which in 1966 had the audience on one side. It was made into a theatrical space.

SW: Are you getting invited by theatres to present your work and, if so, do you want to show your work in theatres?

YR: Who invites me? Museums now. We will be performing at the Louvre. A comparable situation was several years ago when I had a retrospective exhibition, similar to but larger than Raven Row, at the Kunsthaus Bregenz, a big modern museum. And right next door was a classical theatre, where my group performed. It was like Raven Row only they performed only one night or two nights rather than a month. Raven Row was more like a Broadway or off-Broadway run! Our rehearsals for the new work at MoMA are taking place when the museum is closed. That is another thing. We have limited time to rehearse. There is no such thing as a sit down static audience during the day in any one of these galleries because there are people constantly wandering around. This is the reason that museums are thinking more about theatrical spaces in their expansion plans.

SW: Who is the curator at MoMA that you are working with as part of the commission for your new performance work?

YR: Ana Janevski and Stuart Comer, the MoMA curators of media and performance, are coming up to speed. Ana is travelling around looking at a lot of dance. And I am getting everything I need. I am hiring a pianist. I'm also using a painting from the collection, which will travel on a dolly.

SW: Can you talk more about that?

YR: It has a history. MoMA commissioned Ralph Lemon to organise a series of events: dance and panels and discussions around the central theme of 'Value.' He invited me to do something. I said I would go to sleep under Henri Rousseau's painting, *The Sleeping Gypsy*. It was one of my favourite pieces in the museum when I came to New York in my early twenties. I planned to take a sleeping pill and sleep for six hours or however long the museum was open. I did not even know that two years earlier Tilda Swinton had gone to sleep in a glass case at MoMA and I thought, "Well, that is very different from what I am going to be doing because I will have a handout which talks about the relative, comparable value of the painting and my sleeping body underneath." This aging inert dancer. We were going back and forth about this and then I googled 'Tilda Swinton at MoMA' and saw this photograph of the glass case and people with their noses pressed up against the glass ogling the sleeping celebrity. And I thought, "Oh my god, people are not going to necessarily read this one page handout. It will just be another voyeuristic exercise," which I do not find interesting. So I pulled out of that. Meanwhile, MoMA had invited me to do this performance and Ana actually encouraged me to get *The Sleeping Gypsy* into the performance in some way. So I asked to borrow the painting and will invite a couple of handlers to pull the painting on a dolly slowly from one side of the space to the other for about 20 minutes. I am also having a costume made that resembles the one in the painting. It is one costume and every night one or two people will alternately put it on whenever they like and take it off.

I didn't think I could get the painting. In a meeting with the curators I described the project to Ann Temkin, the painting curator. She responded, "I can't say no to you." I nearly fell off of my chair! The painting is in.

SW: Will the handlers rehearse as performers?

YR: Yes, it is coming up. We will have a rehearsal. The handlers will be credited in the programme.

SW: It really is a brilliant idea to pull this painting through your work and reference it through costume. Perhaps there is a way for choreographers to think of how to insert the museum into their work not just their work into the museum.

YR: I hadn't initially thought about it that way. It was kind of a serendipitous evolution.

SW: Did the text of yours that was to be used in the sleeping piece get published?

YR: No it hasn't. I will think about adapting it for the performance and hand it to the audience.

SW: As a dancer who has performed in the gallery and museum I can identify with the concern you expressed about performing the sleeping piece, in regards to being looked at as 'the other' or the 'exotic'.

YR: Well, the good thing about Raven Row is that it didn't feel like a museum. The two galleries where the performances took place were empty. There was nothing on the walls.

SW: Who negotiates conditions for your work with MoMA?

YR: Me, to some extent. The financials are handled by Performa, which acts as a sort of agent for me. One reason I left dance for filmmaking was that I didn't want to institutionalise myself with the trappings of a staff, fundraiser, manager, board members and all of that. I don't like to be the person who hands out the cheques to my dancers and the 1099 tax forms and all of that. So it is a convenience for me to work with Performa, which takes 5%. So I am fortunate that way. They are not a management agency. I am one of the few people they handle.

SW: Were you presented with or did you negotiate a budget with MoMA?

YR: I worked out a budget with Performa and then they negotiated with MoMA. It's worked out.

SW: Why does dance want the museum?

YR: OK, that's a very good question. It's validation beyond the dance world. And the problem has been that we feel so indebted and privileged to be invited into a museum. I didn't think about this when I performed in museums in the 60s and early 70s. The Whitney Museum of American Art produced a series of ex-Judsonites and music with Meredith Monk and Philip Glass...Trisha Brown, of course, and Deborah Hay. I don't remember what we were paid or what those arrangements were. I would give my eyeteeth to remember. I don't even know if they kept a record of our being there. We didn't make demands. There was a curator, Stephen Weil, whom we dealt with. I presented work there in two consecutive years. There were removable walls that could be rearranged. I showed the first rough-cut of my first film, simultaneously while the live dance was going on. It was no big deal. It was an available space. It has become a big deal because more museums are doing it and the dancers and choreographers are becoming more savvy about what they need, both financially and physically.

SW: Do you think the museum had the same kind of status for the dance artist then as it does now?

YR: My generation were more integrated with the art world. Our ideas came out of art world ideas such as Minimalism and Pop Art. We were conscious of coming out of a more embraced and cohesive avant-garde. The visual artists were dancing and performing with the dancers. The artists who were a part of Judson, with the exception of Robert Rauschenberg, were not that well known or successful yet. All that seemed to change in the 80s and 90s. Now these worlds seem much more separate and autonomous than they were back then. And since then, economically, the art world has exploded. So, I guess, unless you make demands now you feel like a step-child.

In 1968 I rented the Anderson Theatre on Second Avenue for *The Mind Is a Muscle*. The project was financed with a Guggenheim Fellowship. I needed a traditional theatre because I wanted to fly things. Things went up and down: several swings and a big grid that extended from one side of the proscenium to the other. You cannot do that in a museum. And even in the black box that the new Whitney Museum installed, you won't be able to do that.

SW: Do you have a lighting design for your new work at MoMA and, if so, what is possible in the space?

YR: There is no lighting grid, of course, in the fourth floor gallery where we'll be performing. I work with a lighting designer, Les Dickert, and he's used to working with what's available. He demands and tries to get the most from the situation. Simone Forti did something in the same space at MoMA: she had the existing ceiling lights covered with red gels. The whole room had a red glow. But Les will be bringing in some extra lights. At Raven Row we performed during the day, so there was no special lighting or need for lighting design, which was nice, because I always prefer a bright space.

SW: Do you have any suggestions, based on your experiences and what you have seen, for the next generations of dance artists who may find themselves performing in the spaces of the museum and gallery?

YR: Well, demand your rights. Don't let yourself be exploited, and get as much out of the situation as you can in terms of available spaces. Demand a sprung floor. You know, I don't put down the idea of dancing in front of paintings. The greatest potential now for dancers in museums is that the choreographer has a choice of spaces, right? From a standard theatre to a cubby hole.

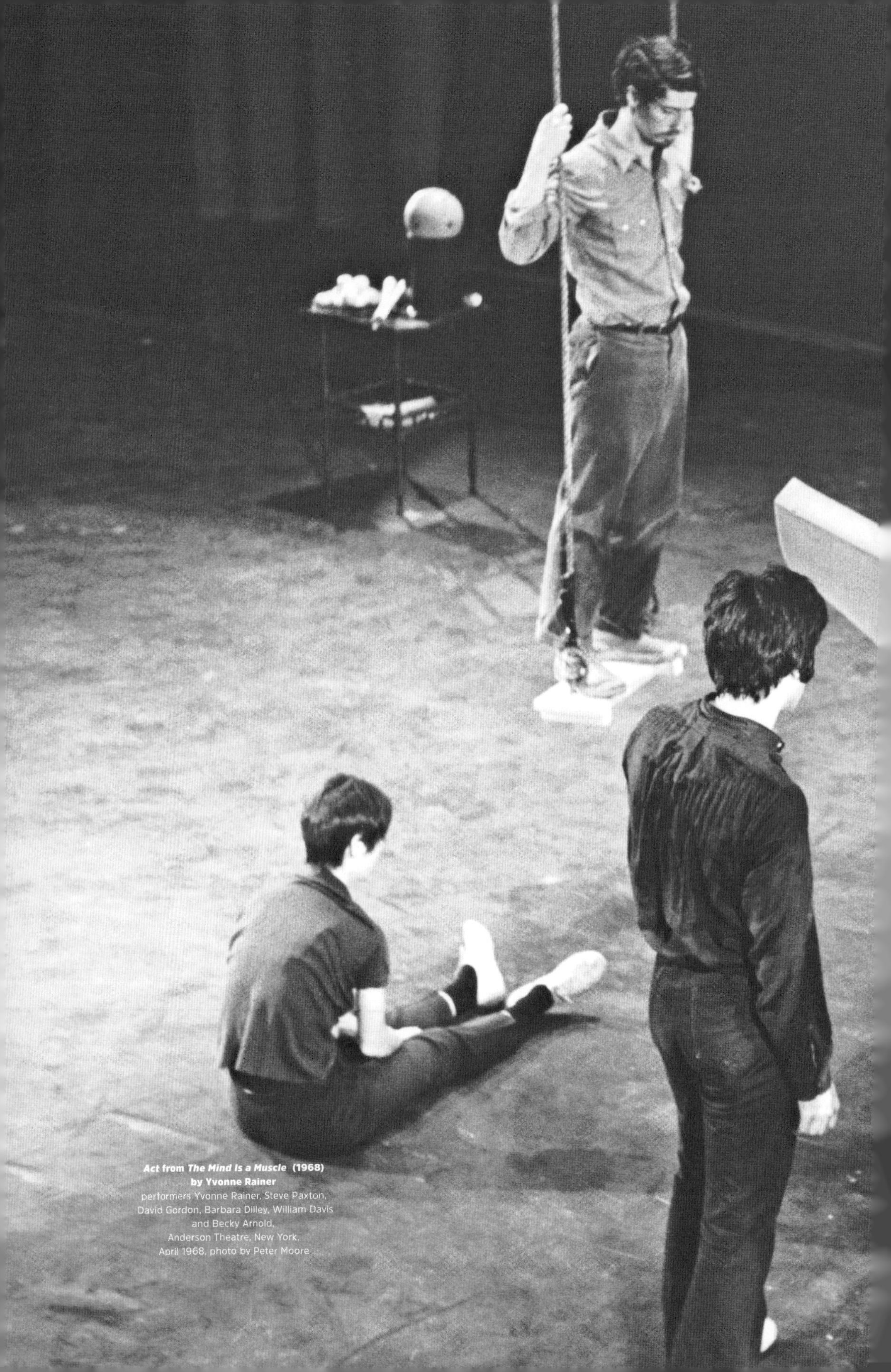

***Act* from *The Mind Is a Muscle* (1968)**
by Yvonne Rainer
performers Yvonne Rainer, Steve Paxton,
David Gordon, Barbara Dilley, William Davis
and Becky Arnold,
Anderson Theatre, New York,
April 1968, photo by Peter Moore

Frank Bock

Freelance Curator

SW: What dance in the gallery or museum project would you like to speak about and can you talk about your role as a curator within it?

FB: I was thinking about *Volumes Project*, which was part of *MIRRORCITY* at Hayward Gallery in 2014. I seek curation as an extension of artistic practice. So it's about fulfilling a set of conditions or opportunity, and to respond to that, not necessarily to the other works in the exhibition. Dealing with time...dealing with relationship...dealing with concept...dealing with collaboration; it feels very similar to making work. It feels like it is making work: making work happen through another form. The show was only made because all of the dancers put into it and are also co-authors of the work. But, actually, that is not how it works. That is often how we talk about it.

The world is stacked up in a very particular way in relation to who is leading something, who is fronting something. So curatorial practice perhaps allows for that stacking to be played with, in a way; it feels a little like an artistic practice that accounts much more for the works involved and the roles of those works... an artist's take, and how they claim space in a certain way. With *Volumes Project,* we were approached by Stephanie Rosenthal. She approached Martin Hargreaves, Nicola Conibere and myself separately. Stephanie wanted to have a spectrum of art forms represented in the *MIRRORCITY* exhibition. Then we were invited to propose dance work that added into the theme of the exhibition; namely what alternative realities the body could open up and the encounter might offer between the spectator and work. We decided to make a project out of it and invite artists to work collectively.

Nicola was definitely going to perform, and she wanted Martin and me to propose work. We had the question, "Do we make ourselves into a collective and invite all of these artists to be part of the collective?" And, "How are we going to structure the work?" We then thought a project was better than the collective. The three of us would co-propose the strand. It was complex because we were the invited artists, so the other five that we drew into the project weren't people that Stephanie had chosen.

SW: What has been your experience in negotiations around the needs of dance artists in the gallery or museum?

FB: That was complicated to navigate because there was a time when our three names were much more visible than the other five. We had the signage changed because they were just listed as 'works' and we had the artists' billing. The five artists we invited to join us were then put up in the text with our billing. There were other collectives in the exhibition that were not named as individuals. There was LuckyPDF, an artist collective, who were named as a collective. We were also keen that the dance artists were named. This felt important for dance to hold its presence alongside the other work. Hence the very interesting negotiation around signage and names. I think the whole exhibition had lots of different configurations of individuals in there, as well as lots of names.

SW: What, from your perspective and experience, does being in the gallery or museum do for dance?

FB: It is always different when you put bodies into a space of objects. What is the offer? How does presence insist itself in a place where there are a lot of objects? How does performance presence insist? I thought *Volumes Project* was successful, although we did not have a designated space. For me, I thought that the dance works were very present, because they also moved around and opened space up. You could meet them in different places.

SW: How did you work within the constraints of the gallery to meet the needs of the dance artists for three months within *Volumes Project* and as part of *MIRRORCITY*?

FB: Dance involves subjectivities in a way that other works don't. There was sometimes a fear I noticed when raising issues around need; that you were falling into kind of over-emotionality, because you are dealing with bodies and concerns and real problems of laundry, etc...These needs seem to have a different kind of relational intimacy than dealing with, say, some technical things not working any more. Dealing with people lends itself to very different kinds of dialogue and power positions.

The project was pretty self-managing. We tried to go in, as much as possible, to give feedback. I think having a production manager would have been really great. We do not have that role in the gallery. Sometimes we would speak to the technical staff at the Southbank Centre – nothing to do with the gallery – for their expertise, because in the installation we weren't able to access support from the gallery. They were behind, they had so much to do. I don't think they anticipated we'd have any technical needs at all. Having a production manager that is dedicated to taking care of the work within the institution would be really good. We had a lot of support from Stephanie's assistant, though she had many others to take care of.

There were times when we tried to arrange technical meetings. The technical people didn't show up...from what I understand...technical support from theatre is different from technical support from galleries. They do not have the 'The Show Must Go On' mentality, because there isn't a show in the same way. If the art object will always be there, it doesn't have that 'make it happen' thing that maybe theatre has.

It's rare to get a chance to present for three months, to present for 82 days. It's great, also, to see how work can evolve in that time. Seeing how the dance artists interacted with the gallery assistants; they shared something that was constant. The gallery assistants see and know the works most – although they are not allowed to talk about the work, strangely – and share the mess room together. They have a certain kind of knowledge about the work. It was nice. The thing that maybe we missed was not seeing the other artists. There was not that much contact with the other visual artists. It seemed that they were just there for the opening and then were gone. So you don't have that sort of collectivity that you might...in a festival you become aware of the other people who are out there, whatever their kind of field is. Whereas in a gallery space you don't get to see them, or you might see the people who've been making the things that the artists have commissioned them to make in their name.

SW: Can you speak about the reason that *Volumes Project* was focused on presenting 'practices' and not finished 'pieces' or 'works' by the invited dance artists?

FB: All of the works that we put in were practices, though they weren't pieces.

They were "works" but they were also ongoing practices. Artists did them whether there were spectators or not, and were interested in the constant iteration of the practice. Whatever they had to deal with was also something they had to incorporate. We were interested in the spectator so we chose a group of artists who all have practices. The only thing that we actually saw before, that was kind of a work, was Neil Callaghan and Simone Kenyon's piece, *Refractions*, but that was still a practice that they kept developing. That allowed us to be responsive with the set up.

SW: Did you facilitate any dialogue between the dance artists in *Volumes Project* and the visual artists in the *MIRRORCITY* exhibition?

FB: It felt important to us that the other artists exhibited in the exhibition knew about us and were asked how they felt about the presence of performance, or these practices, next to their works. Often the reasons were very pragmatic... some said yes, some said no, which is absolutely right. Things can inter-affect each other very powerfully. Things sit in relation to each other, and that needs protecting and respecting. We were also aware, because performers move through the space, that they don't have any signage. The dancers move in front of other people's signs and implicate themselves into other people's work very easily. That was fun to watch; the way that the implied happened.

We had signage downstairs by the entrance, so our signage was prominent. We knew that we wanted more clarity about who was on when. There was a system with rings where you could see who was on when and on what day; I think that only happened halfway through the three months, though. Actually, it would have been nice to have had something like a notice in the foyer each day. We didn't want it to be listed as an event because they were ongoing artworks; when you turn something into an event it becomes different. I don't think it was quite resolved.

SW: Is there anything, in retrospect, that you would have done differently with *Volumes Project*?

FB: I think one should have been able to buy a ticket to the exhibition and come back to see it six times. We were only on six hours a day and the exhibition was open eight or ten hours a day. We were trying to say we were there all of the time. Of course, we were not there all of the time, but we were there every day. To programme something for 82 days is a long time, and we wanted to make sure we fulfilled it. Fitting a time was a concern. How do you administer a schedule like that if somebody cannot do a certain day? So we made it self-organising. If you missed a day, you had to find someone else from the project to cover. There was a time when we thought, in *Volumes Project*, that we could have 'loose leaves'; that we could drop other people in...people who we were interested in presenting. But that didn't work because of signage.

We had a moment – a mid-point weekend – where artists were talking about the exhibition and we were scheduled to have a discussion. That was a shame because that was an opportunity that didn't really happen so well, because they programmed another visual artist speaking at the same time about their work. Hayward didn't integrate us into the visual artists' platforms. They thought we would be drawing on our own networks, who would come to our talk but hardly anyone came to the talk. It was a pity. So you suddenly realised there is still this idea of separation; that we are still doing this specialist thing with a specialist audience. And I think they realised that they hadn't thought that through properly. It didn't feel like we were on a different hierarchy...it didn't feel like we were lower...just, sort of, different.

SW: Did you have an idea about how *Volumes Project* would interact with the space of the gallery and the public, or not?

FB: We had an idea. We knew that the dance artists were going to find their own spaces and their own relationships to the spectator. I was interested in the different kinds of ethical relationships when you encounter a body, as opposed to encountering an object. Sometimes when I see dance work or performance work in galleries, I feel like I have to stay and I don't want to stay. I feel guilty. I can feel all kinds of things that aren't very freeing. When you encounter another body...it becomes an ethical relationship...we wanted to find things that could just be on their own track.

We did that through practices; dance artists who could be in relationship but didn't need the relationship. It wasn't about a promise, or a certain kind of encounter that wasn't so hermetic. So they were not super-interiorised but somehow also available in different kinds of ways.

The other thing we were very insistent upon is that we had a space built in the exhibition for the dance artists which was there from the start. It was an 'off' space, so they didn't have to go to a dressing room anywhere else. They could disappear into the walls of the exhibition and come back out again. It was built with curtains and it was upstairs next to the Susan Hiller artwork. It was a soft space. There was a yoga mat and there was a lockable trunk in it. It was quite big. Four people could be in there quite easily. And it was just theirs. Public could not go in. It was *in* the exhibition. Although they were in-between spaces, operating within in-between spaces, they had their own space (that was important) within that. We were very clear about that from the beginning in the exhibition design, and that it was incorporated. Quite a few of the dance artists didn't use it at all. But it felt symbolic. We wanted it in the gallery. That was something that we envisaged as being important. So if anyone was performing six hours per day, they could just disappear and re-appear again as they needed to. That disappearing, the 'on' and the 'off' space, was also something they could really work with. I think that is something they didn't need in exactly the same way that we imagined.

SW: What did you most enjoy about co-curating *Volumes Project*?

FB: It was really nice to be invited, and then to be able to introduce the artists' work to new people. 24,000 people came to the exhibition which is quite something. What that does for the art form, I don't know. But hopefully it contributes in some way. People are not there, necessarily, to see performance work. Those six practices or six artists...their names within all of those other names, some of them very known...some less known. The visibility was great.

SW: Did Stephanie know about your curatorial practice and approach before contacting you to co-curate *Volumes Project*?

FB: She knew about Independent Dance and my work there. I think she spoke to Eva Martinez, chair of Independent Dance's Advisory Group, who connected us. There was an expertise Stephanie knew she didn't have. I think she had gone around to 70 different artists' studios in London to try and find London artists that she was interested in so she just couldn't take on the dance world. She wanted some people who had particular links to what is happening in dance.

SW: What process did you three use to select dance artists?

FB: We drew on our knowledge rather than going to do the search. We had a lot of approaches from people who knew we were doing that. Once we had an idea of the way their practices might be in the space, we knew we wanted it defined, in a way, the group that we already had. There were more people we couldn't include, and the selected group are pretty similar as a generation. One of the ideas suggested by the gallery was to work with students. It seemed like this was a way of solving the cost of labour by using unpaid students. We had to raise money separately. We got a fee from the Southbank Centre, but it was not enough to have work there all the time. We applied for Arts Council England money and so two-thirds of the money came from money that we brought in. We were talking about extending the invitation in ways that could never be made possible, and it felt important to the art form to increase dance's visibility.

***I am a Robot* (2014)**
by Charlie Morrissey
performer: Charlie Morrissey,
part of *MIRRORCITY: London artists on fiction and reality*, Hayward Gallery, London,
13 October 2014–4 January 2015,
photo by Michael Brzezinski

TIM

Martin Hargreaves

Writer and Dramaturg

SW: What is most exciting for you about your role within projects that present dance in the gallery or museum?

MH: *Volumes Project* was interesting because Stephanie Rosenthal contacted me as I'd been the point of contact for *Move: Choreographing You*, an exhibition at Hayward Gallery about art and dances from the 1960s. She was interested in my locating students from Trinity Laban to work on activating some of the sculptural works. It was an idea in which she wanted to get student workers to come and be in the gallery all day, every day, and interact with Mike Kelley's work. She was also interested in *Trio A* by Yvonne Rainer, because I had worked on the construction of it at Laban. That piece was going to be a work performed every Saturday in the gallery as part of *Move*, for which I had to collect a group of different people. Eventually it changed because she invited Xavier Le Roy and Mårten Spångberg in to make a work with the dancers that were actually alumni from Laban. It very quickly became apparent that Stephanie was asking for a lot, because the dancers were performing in the gallery all day, every day. It had to be alumni because the students couldn't integrate the time into their study, and so it had to be people who were paid. Also, Xavier and Mårten stepped in and made a work on them, so it became a different proposition.

So my process with that was really setting up different meetings or facilitating the reconstruction of *Trio A*. Pat Catterson, one of the certified transmitters of *Trio A*, came over and did all of the corrections, so for me it was more about getting casts together. I set up an audition for Mårten and Xavier because they didn't know London-based dancers, but in the end everyone was a Laban alumnus, partly because that was my community. I think the shift over to bringing in alumni was that they were paid, but not particularly well.

SW: What was the reaction when you had to bring up the fact that they were doing a lot of work and that they needed to be paid? Was that difficult negotiation?

MH: I think, in principle, that the will was there. I think it was just that I started to understand that galleries have very different systems of funding.

SW: Are you distinguishing between volunteers and students?

MH: Yes – I think students who volunteer do so for an exchange that is pedagogical; that it's not placed within the teaching institution, but there is a sense in which it is voluntary. It's not compulsory for these students to do this outside of their usual classes, but they have an interest in starting their professional artistic career; it's then not student labour.

I think that *Volumes Project*, which was in *MIRRORCITY* at Hayward, was the most revealing project in terms of illustrating the practical gaps in understanding that you asked about originally. Frank Bock, Nicola Conibere and I were curating a strand within the exhibition, and there was an idea that the dancers would be self-sufficient within the exhibition, but self-sufficient with support. We spent time communicating with Stephanie and with her assistant about what we needed, not just in advance of the opening but throughout the whole run, and things, sometimes, were not met. For example, simple things in terms of access to space. We'd worked with the architect to create a space within the gallery where dancers could retreat, and that was a private space so they could warm up in advance and did not have to do that somewhere else and come over into the gallery, and that we could keep water in there. Often, within the first few weeks, the dedication hadn't been fully communicated with everybody so things started to be stored in there because they thought it was useful space. So artists would arrive and, instead of having space for their yoga mat, they would have to negotiate ladders and things stored in there.

Another example was with Nicola's work *Do-Re-Me* – which has fabric that the two dancers are rolling in and envelope themselves in, and which needed laundering, which Hayward agreed to launder. After each performance, Hayward would contract out someone to do the laundry, which was great, but actually it never happened on time. Often the dancers would turn up and it would be wet or it wouldn't be there. It was simple on-the-ground project management. I think what we needed was, from our side, someone to be maintained as a project manager. Even on a very sort of rudimentary level. But it seemed like we couldn't pass over the day-to-day running to the gallery because they are not used to that. They are not used to actually managing live artworks.

> **SW:** Is there a certain project that you could share that illustrates the communication links between choreographer, curator and dancers?

MH: I think with *Move* it was definitely in my role to communicate. We were working on thinking through how these students could be in the space, and then it became clear that, actually, if they wanted people all day, every day, I would have to understand what kinds of demands those students, those artists, would need. They would need separate space, lockers, somewhere to keep their stuff, and access to showers. Basic communication. I am sure Hayward must have had live performers in there at some point prior to this, but this was a substantial commitment. A lot of it is just establishing initial parameters.

Another example is the Raven Row *Yvonne Rainer: Dance Works* exhibition, where I was brought on quite early on. Even though a lot of the discussions were with Pat Catterson and Yvonne Rainer, who know what dancers need, I think they wanted somebody from London. I don't know why I was brought in so early for these Skype conversations, because a lot of the insistence on payment, for example, clearly came from Yvonne. There was never any thought that it would be students for that work.

> **SW:** So the team at Raven Row always assumed it would be professional dancers that would either be selected or brought in by someone who knows more than they do about the dance community here?

MH: Yes; I think it was the issue that they wanted people who already knew *Trio A*. They knew that we had done this reconstruction project from the score of *Trio A* at Laban. So they wanted to access that community of dancers.

The rate of pay was not put to me. I was asked how much people were paid in different situations. For example, how much people were paid for *Move*, because I ended up being a performer for Tino Sehgal, as well. After that, we began negotiating around that in terms of other kinds of support, for example laundry and access to kitchens. Alex Sainsbury, Director of Raven Row, was interested in talking to me about dance floors as he hadn't really understood that we would need one so was in touch with our production department at Laban. These were the sorts of conversations going on. Some of these conversations are not very formal, because you are spending a lot of time together on the run-up to an exhibition.

SW: Do you sometimes play a curatorial consulting role?

MH: Because Catherine Wood knows I have an interest in Yvonne's work she would discuss some of the possibilities in terms of the works that we would choose to work on. Of course the final decision was always going to be Yvonne's, but just in terms of my being interested to do something that hadn't yet been reconstructed. Which is why we went for *Diagonal,* a work of Yvonne's made in 1963.

SW: How do you negotiate a fee for that?

At first, when Alex asked me how much my fee was, I said that I do these things for free, because historically I always have. For example, I didn't get paid for *Move.* I very rarely get paid for things like this. I was thinking for the Raven Row show that I was really interested in Yvonne's work and just wanted to see it happen.

SW: There comes a point when you might think that your expertise is worth something. At what point do you turn around and instigate that?

MH: Catherine was great. She publicly said, "No, you need a fee." She turned to me in the meeting and said no. I went away thinking that if I am under-selling myself, by doing so I am under-representing the needs of dancers.

During the first conversations around *MIRRORCITY* with Stephanie, it was clear that there wasn't much of a budget and that they would be interested in using students for the work. Also there was no budget to pay me, and a suggestion that as I had a full time job, the time could be absorbed within this as research or professional development. I had to explain that I don't have research hours as part of my work. The conclusion was that I worked together with Nicola Conibere and Frank Bock to apply for an Arts Council England grant.

SW: What would your ideal role and project be?

MH: It is difficult, as all of the projects I have been involved in are because I am interested in them. It is partly a passion, but also it's about thinking that if I am able to facilitate great opportunities for dancers as an artist, I am OK to do that. One of my fears is that, because there is so little money for these kinds of projects, or people don't realise, actually, how much they cost, I do not want to take money away from dancers. If I have a full time job, and I could somehow integrate this into just what I do, then that is OK, if it means the dancers are being paid.

It felt like it was very important at this moment to work with Yvonne while she is still interested in putting on a show like this. Also because I have worked with Catherine on several occasions to look at *Trio A*. When Catherine was writing *The Mind is a Muscle*, she came to Laban and looked at how we were reconstructing it from the score, and then we did it again in the Tate Tanks and then at Hayward. Both of us, coming from different disciplines, have real interest in Yvonne's work. I was just happy to be a part of it.

I think there are multiple things happening simultaneously, for me. One is that even though I was born in the 1970s, I am very nostalgic for the 1960s because it was a time when dance and, I mean dance and choreography, was speaking to other art forms. A short period in the 1960s where people were able to kind of understand choreographic propositions, who were coming from multiple art perspectives. And often it feels like...working in dance...that dance feels like a poor expressive cousin.

There is a certain kind of excitement because now there are broader discussions around dance. It reinvigorates dance. It also points to the kind of relevance of choreography. I worry that I am placing too much on external validation. Just because the Tate likes something doesn't mean it's good. It's kind of a battle in myself, of wanting these other art forms to validate us whereas, actually, I have a true belief in dance and choreography as being interesting, viable art forms. It's not that we need museums to validate us. So I have an excitement about the moment and also a kind of caution. Also because I wonder whether this is just a momentary kind of appropriation that won't be sustained. It is expensive to sustain, and the need to *produce* works in the museums is going to be very costly. The Whitney Museum of American Art's commitments to Michael Clark and to Sarah Michelson, for example, and now Trajal Harrell, is really exciting because they are understanding that it's not just about moments where you bring somebody in, but it's saying that the thing that dance works with is time...and it works with bodies and everything else. However, it's a completely different model; you don't just buy in the finished work, you invest in it.

Of course, with Yvonne Rainer, Raven Row wasn't funding the production but was having to put money into the reconstruction of her work. And, usually, they don't do that. Even just that is a shift of mind set, to understand the funding and that we need time, space and support. I think it brings in questions of ethics. It brings into question notions of support and how we want to work with each other. You know, there's a cynicism that somehow dance in galleries is about bringing the public in, or kind of creating these spectacles that somehow frame other artworks.

I am not interested in dance being another form of getting people through the door. I am interested in dance as an art form engaging in conversation with the rest of contemporary arts practice. We are these living, insistent beings that respond to social choreography and artistic choreography in multiple ways. I am kind of excited and I am slightly cautious. Is this just another kind of fashion? But some of the curators...and I think Catherine's commitment seems to be very consistent. It's not just about bringing in people who are making work in...like, it makes sense that Michael Clark was at Tate because his whole career has been about engaging other arts practices and he understands the gallery. It doesn't make sense for me when you invite artists who predominantly make work for the theatre and who have no real interest in thinking through the gallery.

> **SW:** Yes, why are dance artists here...I think this is a real interest. Why do the galleries want dance and why does dance want the gallery?

MH: That's a really kind of clear way of putting it. It's not just what we can do for the museum, but what the concept of the museum does for us, which is why I think Boris Charmatz is interesting. What he is saying is that what the museum always does is create a narrative. It invites people to see the contemporary moment through a particular historical perspective. And actually dance often doesn't do that. It's a condensed contemporary moment. It is always this kind of moment of spectacle and it disappears. There is political potential in that, and there are also problems.

***Test Room* (1999)**
by Mike Kelley
choreography by Anita Pace,
performers: Megan Saunders & Andrea Samain,
part of *Move: Choreographing You*,
Hayward Gallery, London,
13 October 2010–9 January 2011
photo by Alastair Muir

Alex Sainsbury

Director,
Raven Row

SW: Shall we begin with how you came to present Yvonne Rainer's work at Raven Row and your relationship to presenting dance and performance in the past.

AS: When Raven Row and curator Catherine Wood started working with Yvonne Rainer for *Yvonne Rainer: Dance Works* (2014), I had not worked with dance before. But Raven Row, which is a non-profit gallery in London, open since 2009, has used performance to animate its programme since it began.

I began to explore performance within an exhibition context when the radio station ResonanceFM set up its studio in a gallery and broadcast live during the course of an exhibition here. Later, artist Suzanne Treister proposed a large-scale exhibition that would include an events programme, involving theoreticians who were also keynote speakers used to addressing conferences about the application of technology in society, especially for political or even military ends. In the end I said I couldn't make the whole exhibition but would be interested to bring over some of these grand public speakers at the time of the London Olympics. I knew this was going to be a lavish gesture, but it seemed to correspond with the mad spending on the Olympics. So we built an auditorium for them in Raven Row like a Greek amphitheatre. The rhetorical and the performative were combined. We also created an exhibition framework for these events which consisted largely of video and archival material.

More recently, Raven Row made an exhibition out of a series of performances and discussions about the relationship between art and contemporary literature. Actually, we have just given a tentative name to this strand of the programme here, which we are calling 'live exhibitions'. Our approach is not necessarily so concerned with performance art per se. We did once host the great performance artist Esther Ferrer, who came to prominence in Spain in the 1970s and is now practically peerless. She performed some of her classic pieces, which were dazzling, pitch perfect and hilarious. Esther is from the time when performance art was most vitally developed: just after the Downtown scene in New York, which included Yvonne Rainer, had brought dance into correspondence with new art practices such as Pop Art and Minimalism.

SW: Can you reflect on, from your perspective, how dance and art practices are engaging more recently?

AS: Since the 1990s, with the advent of so-called relational aesthetics, a desire to elide the space between artist and viewer, and a hybridity across means and media has meant that artists and art institutions have embraced many forms of performance. Anyway, art schools in this country have long fostered the happy idea of the amateur; that artists can be polymaths at work in a variety of disciplines, whether literature, science or indeed performance. Although this can give rise to lacklustre performance works that pale in comparison to experimental theatre or even comedy, some hybrid practitioners (Tino Sehgal comes easily to mind) are successfully changing the way we think about art. And I am aware that plenty of practitioners within dance have also shifted expectations of what an art exhibition can be.

SW: It seems, based on the artists and artworks that Raven Row presents, you have an interest in the socio-political movement of the late 1960s, early 1970s. If this is correct, did this interest factor into your decision to present Yvonne's work that emerged from that time period?

AS: Raven Row often represents art from the past, hopefully thinking in terms of the present. Since the turn of the millennium, when there hasn't seemed so much to look forward to, this approach has seemed increasingly fruitful. Contestation of all kinds was more present in the 1970s, when there was a palpable possibility for change, from giant social/political issues, to smaller concerns about how art might be shown, or galleries and museums be used.

Of course it's generally difficult re-visiting historical live work. Even Yvonne acknowledges that a lot of her historic choreography cannot be made again, but is lost without good enough notation. What seemed important for myself and the exhibition curator, Catherine Wood, was that the archival history of Yvonne's choreography from the 1960s was positioned in direct relationship to a live representation of her work from that period, so that the historical and static material could inform the live choreography and vice versa. We were keen to accumulate the various forms of Yvonne's production, to generate a picture of the huge breadth of her practice, from filmmaking and writing to various forms of dance performance. Catherine also included an empty gallery which played a performance lecture of Yvonne's from the 1960s, identifying her voice as a further means she used.

SW: How do you think the spaces of Raven Row supported the presentation of Yvonne's work?

AS: In the space of an art gallery such as Raven Row, as compared to an auditorium, the effect of Yvonne's choreography becomes especially powerful. Bodies in choreographed movement take on a vitally expressive relationship to the art objects they are replacing, and the 'work-like' movements of Yvonne's choreography argue powerfully for an elision of art with everyday life. Minimalism – the movement that Rainer's work is most associated with – is too easily misread as a formal project, even when enjoying a walk over a floor piece by Carl Andre. But Yvonne's work here represented it as anything but that.

SW: As one of the dancers in *Yvonne Rainer: Dance Works*, I always felt at home in the spaces of Raven Row and that it accommodated us as dancers. I wonder why that was...

AS: Raven Row's architecture, designed by 6a architects, aided the effect of the performances. The galleries have an evenness and openness; walls, ceilings and floors carrying equal weight. Contemporary art galleries at their best, I think, express the idea of a working studio, so should easily accommodate performance. I encouraged 6a to propose a generous opening onto the odd sort of public space that Raven Row looks onto.

SW: Are you referring to the picture window?

AS: Yes, such a picture window might be problematic for museums concerned with light levels, and interfere with some artists' and galleries' idea of neutrality. I think it fits with a modern idea about visual interchange between inside and outside. Yvonne and Pat Catterson, one of the certified transmitters of Yvonne Rainer's repertoire, exploited very effectively the way this window framed a view of people moving on the street behind the performers, in direct parallel with their movements. It was as if there was a screen behind the dancers, even as Yvonne sometimes projected films as a backdrop behind her performances. Yvonne's choreography correlated so perfectly with the movements of the passers-by, especially if they were pushing something or carrying heavy packages. The dancers responded to this propitious situation themselves, opening the window completely during performances, which took place in summer, to absorb the living streetscape into the work.

SW: What do you make of this renewed interest in dance in galleries and museums?

AS: In Yvonne's recent survey exhibitions in art galleries, live performances of her choreography have taken place in neighbouring auditoriums, despite the fact that in the 1960s her work was rarely, if ever, performed behind a proscenium. One issue for museums might be that too few numbers can be admitted to justify the cost of live dance in galleries. Raven Row has never been overwhelmed by visitors, and a project such as this becomes more feasible if you have no more than 150 visitors on any day.

SW: How did you develop a budget for this project?

AS: I had worked out likely costs on the back of an envelope, with much help from the great Martin Hargreaves, who organised the dancers through the Trinity Laban in London. And it seemed expensive but doable. Raven Row is anomalous: not only being privately funded, but also being able to focus its resources on funding exhibitions when other institutions on much higher annual incomes can fork out less for theirs.

SW: Were there any obstacles?

AS: One big obstacle to overcome was persuading Yvonne that the gain of such a direct proximity between performer and viewer was worth the limited room for manoeuvre the dancers would have. Since her return to choreography (after a period out of dance between 1972 and 2000) she has understandably privileged the needs of the dancer. But when she finally visited Raven Row after a long time in discussion, she happily recalled the benefits of intimacy in the days of the Judson Theater, and became enthusiastic. Then Catherine Wood encouraged her to re-work some of her historic material that she hadn't visited for a while...She was still anxious about the capacity of the dancers to perform so regularly over a five-week period. Martin Hargreaves was again reassuring, and insistent that the dancers were quite robust enough for this...

SW: What role, if any, did you feel you played in taking care of Yvonne's work and the dancers in your space?

AS: The role of curator, traditionally, was that of the caretaker. Taking great care of the presentation of Yvonne's work here was such a pleasure...as well as learning how dancers should be looked after. Laundry is not something we usually have to worry about during the course of an exhibition...I will certainly miss the way in which live movement animated the galleries here. Artwork on walls has seemed so inert since then!

***Diagonal* (part of *Terrain*) (1963)**
by Yvonne Rainer
performers: Antigone Avdi,
Alice MacKenzie, Megan Armishaw
& Emelie Wangstedt,
part of *Yvonne Rainer: Dance Works*,
Raven Row, London,
11 July–10 August 2014,
photo by Eva Herzog

Siobhan Davies

Choreographer and Artistic Director,
Siobhan Davies Dance

SW: Can you talk about one work in relation to dance and the gallery or museum?

SD: I thought I'd talk about *Manual*. The initial and vibrant pleasure was that we were commissioned to make a work and show it amongst the work of seven Scottish sculptors. We weren't commissioned to respond to the sculptures, we were asked to make a work for this exhibition in which we would be on equal terms with any other artist in that space. *Every Day* took place at the Gallery of Modern Art in Glasgow (GoMA). Ben Harman, the curator, approached us late in 2012; our event was seen in the summer of 2013. I had made *To hand* in 2011 with Matthias Sperling at Whitechapel Gallery, which was made specifically in response to a Claire Barclay installation: *Shadow Spans*. At GoMA we were invited on our own terms. The theme of the show was 'the everyday'. The audience could make up their own minds how the individual sculpture or our live event might interact with each other. We thought of ourselves as co-existing with the others, but we were all addressing the theme. It was the simplicity and straightforwardness of the invitation which was enticing.

Helka Kaski, the dance artist who I had chosen to work with, and I researched all the Scottish artists, and Ben was very helpful about sending down information. We went up to see the work in Glasgow before we started. Both Helka and I could use this as an opportunity to learn something about the other artists and to read further about the art world's take on the term 'everyday'. The gallery we were going to work in is a vast pillared space on the ground floor, with lots of light coming in from big windows on the long sides. The whole gallery has its own history; once being used as a bank and later a Royal Exchange.

SW: How did you and Helka approach the theme of 'the everyday'?

SD: Helka and I looked at this idea of the everyday and tested various possibilities. I had remembered a moment when I had been involved in a weeklong residency organised by the dance artist Gill Clarke, during which there had been a friendly argument between a philosopher and a scientist. I had asked the philosopher to lie down and the scientist to tell him how to get up off the floor, using detailed verbal instructions. It was a very quick way of asking them to notice something in their own bodies. They achieved this with much laughter and some pain!

SW: Did you prompt that activity to resolve the issue that they were grappling with?

SD: I can't be sure; we were discussing the difference between movements we all know and do unconsciously every day and movements that use more expression. Gill had given everyone, including the philosopher and scientist, a movement class in the morning. I think they were shocked by how much they had enjoyed the experience of thinking and doing in action. My request was quite instinctive, maybe to ask them to notice that what is everyday in action is also oddly unknown to part of us. I think I wanted to share this so fragile network of alliances of which everyday movement is made and also the exploratory nature of dance artists.

Anyhow, I introduced that idea to Helka and we worked with that for a day or two asking each other questions. Testing if it was strong enough as an idea to repeat and rich enough to sustain the interest of the different kinds of visitors to the gallery. During our preparation time we asked 50 people to come and work with us in the studio before we presented the work. Some questions and challenges came up, such as how could we engage confidently with the visiting audience and create an opening gesture which could invite them to help Helka to get up from a lying position on the floor, but only using words, no physical help! The opening gesture we came up with is that Helka would introduce herself to one person and say, "My name is Helka Kaski, and would you help me complete this work?" And then she would set out from that opening sentence and sense how she could be with each different person. We also learnt during the preparation time that it was essential that Helka must not appear passive. She could not allow herself to be treated as a body to be manipulated, but rather that *Manual* was essentially a partnership between her and the person who was helping her to complete the work. That had to be made clear very quickly.

During the preparation period before we entered into the actual gallery space, we needed to work on how Helka could refrain from predicting the next move she would naturally take and, instead, remain with her partner, waiting for the next instruction. She could, however, point out where her weight was, or where the direction of a movement might serve, or where there was a strain, so that through conversation the action would be able to continue. To me there was a particular virtuosity in how Helka remained so accurate and alive in the positions she moved into and held for quite a while. In stillness, these moments, isolated from a flow of action, were a beautiful glimpse of how our bodies are at work.

One of the things that spiralled out from both the preparation and residency in the gallery was how crucial the conversations were, each one different, but centered on this simple movement we all share. The revelation that some members of the audience felt when they had accomplished the task was really good to witness. They had gone through a gamut of emotions: perplexity, frustration, joy. You can't imagine the number of people who embraced Helka when she finally got up, and some of the dialogues continued afterwards.

> **SW:** Can you say more about the kind of equality that you were looking for in the space of the museum?

SD: I am not sure about looking for equality. It feels more like creating situations in which different ways that works or artists can thrive. In *Manual* we had a double sense of being side by side. One where *Manual* kept company, had equality if you want, with the other works in the exhibition and one where Helka was the companion to someone willing to engage with her. It did not take long for the visitor to forget the circumstances and join Helka fully in what the task was. I found it very striking when, without them knowing, their bodies with very different histories and expectations echoed each other while they were trying to work out a piece of shared action.

The dialogue between the visitor and Helka was mostly private. The gallery space was enormous. Although people did sit and watch or stand and watch, the engagement between Helka and the other person became very compressed and condensed. The first 30 seconds to a minute, the visitor would have a moment of questioning why they were doing it, slight embarrassment, a shock, actually, when they had to start. Within a minute, you'd find that they didn't notice anything other than what they were doing and what Helka was doing. They saw or heard nothing else because they were so immersed.

> **SW:** How important was it to you going in that there would be an audience, or to be thinking about the audience?

SD: We did think about it, but it was something we hadn't practised. We practised the clarity of the engagement, and we tried to put ourselves in as many different situations as we could with as many different genders, ages, expectations and fears of the 50 people during the preparation. Then it did become very different in the actual space – different because we were with the other works, and the visitors arrived with no knowledge or intention to take part, whereas, in the studio, each person knew a little about our project.

One extra and delightful memory was that Helka is Finnish and the Glaswegian accent is fairly robust. So I even asked a doctor friend of my son's, who has a very strong Glaswegian accent, to come and have dinner with us the night before to be sure that she could be understood, or that he could be understood by her! In the end, none of those fears came into being. We tried to prepare ourselves as well as we could. We had a bench, and Helka sat on it. Helka had a really clear posture. I tried to imagine a member of the audience coming in and seeing her clarity amongst these other works. She would stand up, approach them and say, "My name is Helka Kaski, would you help me complete this work?" Not knowing what would happen, the surprise of a person being invited, and then, thank goodness, the first few times, everybody said yes. There was a variation of behaviour in the public who weren't interacting with Helka; some people slightly hiding behind a pillar to watch what was going on, or others gathering and looking at this work before moving on to another of the sculpted works, or some people moving their shopping baskets down and sitting. A lot of the time people couldn't hear but they could see the intent, and were able to watch, for as long as they wished, people at work – an everyday activity – in the context of 'the everyday'. Often they would stay for the full duration, or they would go and then return and see how far Helka had risen.

There was an ongoing conversation between the two of us and others: was this a performance or was it not? Helka and I worked out that it was a performance but there was also a presence in her body that was reachable rather than removed; she was both alert to what was going on around her as well as communicating at close quarters. She needed to keep that communicative level throughout the day – she did it for about six hours, and it was very tiring. There were times when people would talk with her afterwards about something quite personal. I don't think that had been our expectation, and we had concerns about whether this was the right way for the work to go. But in the end we thought we could allow it to be what it is but not to let it go on too long, let there be a moment in which Helka could bring it to a close.

SW: I'm trying to imagine how this works in the museum context; pristine and white and full of light...

SD: It was less pristine because it had a previous history. Yes, a lot of light and huge height; it was built to be impressive, with a vaulted and designed ceiling, a rhythm of pillars. Not an intimate space, but the windows allowed us to see what was going on in a busy shopping and cafe area so that seemed to mediate the grandness, but also the gallery and its staff made it feel very welcoming. This enormous gallery sometimes felt like a Mediterranean square with people walking around it in the afternoons. I don't remember the gallery being intimidating.

SW: Your work has moved into museum spaces over the years; do you think about your work as belonging in a gallery or museum or, at times, does it belong in a theatre? Do you get the invitation and then work out how you'll work within that space, or do you make a work and see what kind of space it asks for?

SD: There are definitely a series of conscious decisions made. The companion piece to *Manual* is *To hand*, where Matthias places himself on upturned plastic pots, so his body is suspended a few inches off the floor. By moving each pot to support a different part of his body, he moves himself around the space. This behaviour came about in order to share the space with Claire Barclay's installation. We had talked to her about how she seemed to have captured a stilled moment in the making of an object such as a hat, so that it was not a completed hat but at a turning point of being something else. We wanted to be in a state of continuous decision-making, but we did not want to interfere with what Claire had made. We wished to share the ground and that our action might slow people down enough to both watch and be in this created space.

Those two pieces helped us make the decisions about how to make *Table of Contents* (2014). We learned that to be seen at work, to be seen in concentration, was a good invitation for a visitor to stay. After our experience of *Manual*, we wanted to develop an easy conversation with the audience. Sharing the big tables, which were a feature of *Table of Contents*, made this more possible. Something which intrigued us was the different states of attention needed by the artists towards to the audience. At one moment we might be talking easily and then move towards something more performative but maintain the connection. There were these very subtle shifts that we wanted to learn more about, and the tenderness and the exactitude of how to make these shifts became an incredibly important part of the whole thing.

In *Table of Contents*, we had the audience in mind right from the first day. We wanted to get to grips with why we wanted to be in these gallery spaces. We want to be in a common ground with the visitors. Using that as a base we can explore the different temperatures that might exist between us and the public.

SW: I think the museum allows that because it's a public space.

SD: It is a public space, and the fact that people can come and go means that as a performer you genuinely know where you stand with somebody. I am curious where we dance-based performers might choose to place an internal border between expressing ourselves as an articulate, informed performer and then moving back across to being the source material we always are. How we might decide quickly or hover between these states. It is delicate decision-making, playful. Recently, I am more conscious of how my body is a constant, a sort of home key; I can use its different layers of expression with more accuracy. I am still material, both when I am in the street and when I am performing, the nuances are fascinating. How can I use those different seams of attention more effectively?

SW: One of the things that I glean from *Manual* is that it exposes something very unknown about dance or choreography, which is the rigour and the complexity of the human body and how it organises itself, which could be an appreciation for dance or babies and children, mechanical engineering...

SD: I like that!

SW: Was that a residue that came out of the tasks that you created in the studio or something that you wanted to get across?

SD: I wanted it. I think we got more from the whole process than I might have predicted. One of the initial engines for the work was remembering a radio programme

I had listened to years ago. It was a re-look at the Seven Wonders of the World. People were allowed to introduce their own version. One person presented the wonder of how a human being can stand! That has resonated with me forever. I think I must have started dancing at that point. It was the revelation of the complex orchestration of every movement in the body that continually arouses me.

SW: Because you haven't really talked about the curator, it sounds like you were given free rein to do whatever you wanted.

SD: I was in contact with Ben and sent him up proposals as they were developing and he answered me. I think we had a rich flow of information. He was delightful to work with. His wife was having a baby and it was difficult for him to come down to London so it was easier for us to talk on the phone or email. When we were performing we were introduced to the baby. In a way he was an unforgettable companion, the everyday of our own lives mingling with the making. Ben is now director of Stills, Edinburgh and is curating a show at our Studios in London later in 2015. That feels like a great continuation...

SW: Can you touch a bit on taking care of Helka, beyond the communication, and of the set up, but more in the physical, spatial sense?

SD: We had concerns about a cold concrete floor, which we went and tested. Choosing something for her to wear which had some protective warmth in it was important. In the museum they looked after us very well. We had a space for changing in. We are quite careful about making sure that there's a piece of paper for all the invigilators, so that they had information they could share with the public. We speak to the invigilators before we start. We had an evening where many of the invigilators came and one of them could do *Manual* with Helka. If they felt comfortable, then that ease meant they would come in and say, "Good morning, Helka," and notice where she was in the space, keep an eye out for her. We try and set those partnerships up everywhere. For instance, at Whitechapel the invigilators enjoyed being with Matthias, who worked seven hours a day with very short breaks. I really felt they looked out for him, which was not an experience we had imagined or necessarily expected. But it was tangible how much we felt that they were there. And the curator, Kirsty Ogg would check up on us often. But you can be in situations which are amusing. For example, when *To hand* was shown at The Henry Moore Foundation in Perry Green, they too looked after us beautifully, but the gallery was far from the main space and Matthias was offered the broom cupboard to change in or rest his legs – with the brooms in it! It was all they had, but the thinking had not quite stretched to the fact that Matthias is an animate being, not a thing. However we were well looked after and, again, the invigilators were so attentive. They play an enormous part; they know the space and they know the public. In all of the examples the invigilators would take the initiative to go up to somebody and explain something where they felt there was curiosity.

SW: Taking care and looking after the space, the objects and people.

SD: Another element is choosing what parts of the aesthetic of being in a gallery do we adopt or not; for instance, at Turner Contemporary – another gallery we have a good relationship with – there were things like labelling the work. Actually putting a label on the wall, because we thought we should have a way of identifying what we are doing and keeping it within the expression of the gallery. There are small things. I think there's this gulf when we don't know what question to ask, once we can gather up these questions and expand from there, a lot of what is needed is simple.

***Manual* (2013)**
by Siobhan Davies in collaboration with Helka Kaski
performer: Helka Kaski, part of *Every Day*, Gallery of Modern Art (GoMA), Glasgow, 22 March–1 September 2013, photo by Alan Dimmick, courtesy of Glasgow Life

Hugo Worthy

Exhibition Officer for Contemporary Art,
New Walk Museum and Art Gallery

SW: I am curious to know about how you engage dance at the New Walk Museum and Art Gallery, and some of the things you have to consider when doing so.

HW: As a local authority institution, we're directly managed by Leicester City Council, and they own the artworks. It's publicly funded but the majority of arts provision in the United Kingdom is, primarily, publicly funded. But it's not just publicly funded; it is directly managed by the city. So the City Mayor is, in theory, my boss. And if he doesn't like something, or his councillors don't, then it doesn't happen. And if their constituents are unlikely to like it, it doesn't happen; so local authority museums are instinctively conservative spaces. We're talking about performance art – we had Ron Athey come and give a talk, a little while ago. There was no possibility of him performing because the work is so explicit, so we invited him up to talk, and that was great to have his presence alongside the German Expressionist work. So, there are a range of expectations; political expectations.

The background to our work with Matthias Sperling, a London-based dance artist, was in the redevelopment of our German Expressionist gallery beginning back in 2012. We put in an application to Arts Council England to fund redevelopment of our German Expressionist collection as a key holding of the museum; it had been a little bit neglected, both in terms of how it had been exhibited and how the collections connect. I was involved in the development of the bid, and we inserted this idea of *gesamtkunstwerk*, total artwork, into a reading of German Expressionism, so that the gallery was going to – as a shell – look and function like a gallery, but at its heart was this idea that it would function like a space that facilitates live activity. So, essentially, we were trying to get a very open idea of what liveness might mean. So we began to explore different architectural solutions and design solutions for how we might facilitate or support performance work within the redevelopment of the German Expressionist gallery. We started to look at narratives around German Expressionism, performativity and performance. More or less concurrently we won an award from Contemporary Art Society to acquire a performance artwork as part of this process. This was a real kind of a landmark for us because our collections – we have one media work in our Fine Art Collection… We collect plastic art that's quite traditional to the model of collecting. Suddenly we were electing to purchase in an area that is pretty much a wild frontier at the moment. There are plenty of organisations exploring how this can be done but no standardised best practice models.

SW: What is your relationship to dance and performance?

HW: One of the things that underpins our relationship to dance and performance is that we are not just interested in displaying it, but in how it can enter the collections. Through our conversations with dance artists, performers, or visual artists working in performance, how it can become part of the collection has been a significant question for us, one that we haven't got a single answer for. But we are interested in having this conversation with artists.

SW: Does New Walk own any dance or performance works?

HW: Before we commissioned Matthias, through the Contemporary Art Society scheme, we elected to acquire a performance by Marvin Gaye Chetwynd called *Home Made Tasers*, which was produced for the New Museum in New York and shown in Nottingham. We worked closely with Marvin to develop it into a piece which could become part of the collection and which could be restaged in the future. So that work now belongs to us. During this process we've become really interested in different models, different ideas of performance. I think our starting point was that we were interested in performance arts in the visual arts sector… like Marvin Gaye Chetwynd is emblematic of that in the UK; I guess Marina Abramović is the best known figure. I'm not so excited about Marina Abramović's practice, necessarily, but she's a useful reference point.

We were working through this process with Marvin Gaye Chetwynd. Art Fund had given us some research money and we had been in conversation with Nicola Lees at Frieze. And it was actually Nicola who put us in touch with Kate Coyne at Siobhan Davies Dance. That began the ball rolling in terms of exploring dance as a medium. I don't think it was something that we originally intended to engage with. Running concurrently with that is a very strong department of dance at our local university, De Montfort University, which has Ramsay Burt as the professor there. We became aware that dance was important, and particularly important within German Expressionism. We began to look at the possibility of commissioning a dance work for the opening of the German Expressionist gallery. One of the things talked about in this context is that we wanted a performance work to exist tonally in relationship to the German Expressionist gallery, rather than as an explanation or interpretation. We didn't want it to become a layer of interpretation. We wanted it to be something that stood up as an independent artistic practice reflecting German Expressionists' interest in multi-disciplinary use of studio spaces. So when Kate suggested Matthias, we met up with him and outlined the commission, and part of that was that it did have to be situated directly in the German Expressionist gallery as a performance space, but it didn't have to respond directly to the collection. It just had to physically inhabit that space. And that was useful. He talked about responding to works already partially in development, or developed for the commission. It was a useful first meeting. It set us up for what was going to happen, more or less. One of the challenges for Matthias, and for us, was that it would become a very short time scale. At that point it was about six months before the work would launch in August.

> **SW:** What do you find the differences are in presenting, say, a dance artist compared to a visual artist?

HW: We are knowledgeable within the world of visual arts. We are *not* knowledgeable within the world of dance. That was one of the things that became apparent almost immediately. The set of reference points is different across the board between dance and visual arts. That's not just in terms of the kind of artists that you refer to, or the critics who you are engaging with, or the thinkers. There's some overlap. But the parameters and the business models around how you sustain it, about rehearsals, studio space – all of these kinds of challenges are quite different within the dance world. And the expectations of an artist can be quite different within the world of dance… can be quite different from those of a visual artist. And it's really interesting working across performance – performers with a visual arts background like Marvin, who are used to the gallery context. We were working with Matthias and looking at ways to support his practice. He had a really close, a really good relationship with Siobhan Davies Dance, who'd been hugely supportive of the project and offered him studio space in which to rehearse, and that was interesting because we would never think of supplying studio space for an artist. We don't have that, it's not a thing. You don't supply studio space for a visual artist. It's not part of the process, whereas for a performer it is a part of the process. So that was really interesting for us.

SW: How do you translate dance works into a visual-arts-based environment?

HW: It had come up in a conversation that I'd had previously: I'd gone to Performa in New York and seen a variety of work, primarily from visual arts backgrounds working in performance. Through that process, while I was out there I met up with Travis Chamberlain, who is the Associate Curator of Performance and Manager of Public Programs at New Museum of Contemporary Art. He was great and really useful in terms of coming from a clear-cut performance background and translating that into a visual arts setting, and the challenges around it. He was very clear, particularly about those issues in relation to the expectations of the performer...the business modelling around it...how those are different from a visual artist. There's a model out there which (a) is expensive, and (b) I find problematic in some ways, which is that you translate performance work into a kind of museum model and it becomes durational. It's there as long as the museum is open. It seems to me, there are practices that that works for, or that depend on that, but the majority of performances are events that happen over a period of time and then they're gone, and it completely changes how they function if you have to translate them into some sort of permanent presence in a museum. So one of the things that we were really interested in was how to balance that chronological model of curating that dominates a kind of performance programme, against the spatial model of curating that dominates a museum.

We've done some work with a Museum Studies department near us, University of Leicester Museum Studies, which is one of the world's best Museum Studies departments, weirdly. It was the first one, so it's hugely influential. They like to look at these questions about how museums are shifting away from a spatial model of self-identification and education to a temporal model. So you go in and find the daily events programme now in the front of the museum, and that wasn't something you would find before. That lends itself to performative practices being integrated in a way that doesn't turn them completely into objects or have them once, at seven o'clock in the evening. So that was kind of a challenge for us, and what we had been exploring with Marvin. Then with Matthias it became the opposite...the beginning of the process that we'd missed with Marvin. We hadn't done the commissioning with Marvin, we had something existing that we were translating into a museum assessionable format. With Matthias it was a question of commissioning. Matthias had a relationship to the East Midlands where already he works closely with Dance4 in Nottingham, and he'd worked at Embrace Arts before, which was a local performing arts venue which helped. We wanted to work with an artist who was going to be able to understand the challenges that we had in working for the first time with dance. We were very open. This was not something we were experts in; it was something that we were new to and we were just feeling our way through.

SW: What kinds of dialogues/communication do you engage in with artists such as Matthias?

HW: With some visual artists it helps to have an ongoing dialogue about the practice with the artist, which I enjoy. One of the joys of the job is that kind of engagement. And that was really an important part of the process with Matthias, in fact it was probably more central with Matthias than it tended to be with a visual artist. Matthias spends a lot of time talking through the ideas, the kind of meat of what it is going to be. That was exciting, and part of that was because we needed to talk through how the performance could exist within the gallery.

There was this very interesting and unusual fluidity of conversation between the kind of logistical challenges that came up and the intellectual mapping of the project. So...he was using flamenco shoes. There was a question of marking of our floor, if our floor could deal with the flamenco shoes; but actually then that became part of a much more rigorous intellectual conversation about authenticity and the value of the performance and intentionality of the performer that was key to what Matthias was talking about...whether you use actual flamenco shoes, or an alternative to flamenco shoes, which in some way affects some kind of ontology of authenticity. These small logistical issues became part of ongoing bigger conversations.

It's interesting, again, because within visual arts I often feel, as a curator, the primary role of curator is to shield the artist from challenges. You are trying to present a white box with total flexibility to an artist. You can never do that, but that's kind of what we are aspiring to. Whereas with Matthias, it was much more a negotiation of the particularities of the environment. That wasn't problematic; that was the starting point for it. That was a really interesting way to work and, actually, we have taken that back into our conversations with other visual artists. Rather than saying, "We're going to try and create a white cube for you," we start by saying, "It's a very particular space with a very specific set of parameters that you can work around."

SW: How did the communication and working relationship evolve with Matthias?

HW: Matthias was able to articulate that kind of relationship between the intellectual underpinnings of the work and the logistical parameters. And there are many, many good things about Matthias but, above all, he was outstandingly patient with us. Because we weren't able to do everything he wanted. I have said this about Matthias a few times to other partners: Matthias was the best example I have had of walking the tightrope of having a particular vision and being able to stick to it and requiring certain physical and intellectual elements to be in place to make that vision happen, but being willing to accept when things can't happen and to work around that. It was really rewarding. There was a sense that we had managed to deliver the majority of Matthias' vision and he'd been able to work around the parameters that we had.

His piece began as a project engaging with hypnotism. Working with the idea that hypnosis, as a form of therapy or as a form of therapeutic practice, related to narratives around the tradition of dance; we talked about how that could become something that in some way is cathartic or healing for the work...the German Expressionist work...which had been – both the artist and also the work sometimes – persecuted by the Nazi regime. But, more broadly, a kind of range of narratives that the artwork existed around...traumas or rifts that could be seen as emblematic in different ways through the German Expressionist gallery.

This idea that you could create a ritualised, performative experience which, at one level, the dancer believed would heal. This whole idea of belief was really important. You would have to hold on to the possibility of that idea while watching the dance, and at the same time, obviously, it is absurd. As rational human beings we know there is no clear possibility that somebody could retrospectively change how the work is valued or its status.

That was a starting point that moved through, and again, there was this interesting thing around logistics in reference to hypnosis. It's so interesting that hypnosis comes with a package of health and safety legislation that is *so* complicated that we couldn't see a way that we could manage that. We saw that we could outsource the risk – Matthias takes responsibility for it, essentially – but we couldn't see a way that we could do it within local authority legislation. It was interesting because you have this legislative, bureaucratic issue that we have to manage, and Matthias was very sympathetic with that. And we explored different models and, in the end, he underwent hypnotherapy with a professor at UCL and did some work around that, and then came back to us and it became a real element to the work, which involved hypnotising others, or in fact himself.

SW: These kinds of conversations and practicalities often can affect the work that is created and experienced. I wonder if any of the conversations you and Matthias were having were made public?

HW: These were really interesting, meaty questions which were coming out of the production dialogue that we were having. It was a really useful day when Kate Coyne came in and joined us. For Kate, it's especially about how you communicate the dialogue that Matthias and I were having; that some of it is present within the performance but some of it isn't, and you have to find some other ways to narrate this process. She was also keen for Matthias and I to have a conversation that was publicly available. We were able to do that after the performance on the second night. Matthias is extraordinary, and was able to generate a lot of support from other partnerships. Usually that falls to us with a visual artist. We would assume, if there was going to be other partnership funding, that we would be responsible for generating that. For Matthias, he took that on, he really got the funding and got significant in-kind support from Siobhan Davies Dance and also cash contributions from Dance4. It was really useful for us. Suddenly we had all of these other interesting partners. Through this project we met Paul Russ, Chief Executive / Artistic Director of Dance4, someone we hadn't been in contact with before, and that has become an ongoing conversation for us which has been fantastic. It really pushed us more into that world and it was interesting to get a sense of where the particular crossovers are.

SW: What does dance bring to or do for New Walk?

HW: For me, it breaks down into two almost discrete areas: One is the local authority, funder-friendly answers around accessing new audiences. We get in audiences who would not have gone to a museum to see static performance. For that kind of thing, unless it's really targeted, it's still people who have a fairly strong level of cultural experience. But, that said, it does change the reach of our activities. The second answer is about animating space and responding to histories; art histories in which there was a less heavy divide between forms of cultural practice. That historically dance did take place alongside German Expressionist painting within the studio-cum-gallery space. The idea that now we'd only have paintings or drawings of dance – but dance actually taking place seemed to us to make sense.

New Walk is not an exclusively contemporary art museum but it is anomalous in terms of how German Expressionists' work would have been perceived originally, to have it in a static, clinical museum setting. So, for us, it was about changing the dynamics in which the museum works. One of the areas that we worked in a lot is around children and young people and about how contemporary art practice can provide a point of access for them, and consistently throughout that is how we talk about the re-opening of modes of physical engagement with space. We did a show called *Play Ground* in 2011. It ran from Duchamp to the present day. The piece I will refer to was by a guy called Mungo Thomson, who is a Californian conceptual artist. He does these inflatable versions of art galleries in New York, so important small places in New York. And then it became James Turrell's sky spaces. They are inflatables, so you can go in and bounce; it's really nice. As the artist says; there's loads of conceptual meat you can chew on, or you can just bounce.

SW: Can you talk more about your interest in engagement, as suggested by what you just shared?

HW: Museums as we know them came into being in the Enlightenment period. There is this idea from this period, that material knowledge is static and can be held still, which still absolutely dominates the museum sector. The idea that because you happen to have a bowl that is a hundred years old and you pull it out and show it, it doesn't mean that it's the same thing. It's changed completely, through the context as well as physically.

For me what seemed important there was the idea that you have an option of not engaging in a traditional museum way with the museum's objects, and that motion is a really important part of that process of engagement. So the starting point for the exhibition was this provocation from the medieval origins of the museum: the church is the model for the museum, but what would have happened if, culturally, the fairground – which was kind of parallel to the church in the medieval period – had become the model? This idea of physical play and engagement, which a few artists have started to revisit during the late 20th century, is a legitimate way of engaging culturally, as opposed to the idea that only cerebral engagement is a mode of engaging with cultural practices. So we got really into that, and out of that came our ideas of performativity and participation. When we talk about performance work we talk about it as a fairly expanded field, so that I would talk about artists producing workshops for young people as a performative practice. Some of them wouldn't actually, it's interesting.

SW: Tell me more about your purchasing live works...

HW: For now, I'm thinking about the Marvin Gaye Chetwynd piece that we bought. It was first presented to us as a sculpture called *Brain Bug*, valued at £30,000 through Sadie Coles' gallery. Which was fine, that is exactly the budget that we had available. That was OK. But what we wanted to buy was a performance. Fundamentally what happened was that we bought that sculpture with a performance thrown in.

It is really interesting. There really isn't a model for collecting performance out there. Tate collects performances. They have what are fundamentally instructional works, which are really tightly defined and reproducible; for example, Roman Ondák's *Good Feelings in Good Times.*

One of the challenges with dance, and this comes out in Marvin's work as well, is that there isn't necessarily an intent to create a precise physical replication from one staging to the next. For Matthias and Marvin it was about intentionality. I think that what's important to me about this kind of practice is that historically they have disappeared. I am thinking about masques from the 17th century...There's no way to really re-enact them. Museums have a responsibility to try and find ways, not to value the works – the work is already valued through the exhibition process – but to translate it into a format where it could be revisited in the future in a meaningful way. Marvin's practice is hugely important at the moment, Matthias' practice is hugely important at the moment. If we haven't found a way to translate their practice into a museum-friendly model we will have some of the problems that already exist around 1960s activity in terms of people engaging directly with it.

We are the first regional museum to collect performance work. GoMA has a Roman Ondák. I asked Pip Laurenson, Head of Collection Care Research at Tate, about this: is there any equivalent internationally to what we've have purchased? Because in terms of materials conservation it's very complicated for the artwork because Marvin's work is not built to last, but is also not going to translate into being a set of clear cut instructions that are easily replicable. It will need in some sense to be directed each time and there is flexibility for it to change. And Catherine Wood, at Tate, was very clear that they don't make any changes to the production once they have purchased it, whereas Marvin was clear it has to be alive and respond to innovation from performers and audience.

A lot of our conversations with Matthias, particularly, are about documentation and the relationship of the event per se and the event itself. What we have consistently done here is to prioritise the event as the moment for the artist and for the audience which has primacy. We want to enable future audiences to revisit that in a way that the artist is comfortable and happy with and that represents their practice.

SW: Do you present re-staged works at New Walk?

HW: We are re-performing *Home Made Tasers* in April 2015. It has been a kind of ongoing process where she has put together these four hours of instructional videos. This is one of the really fascinating things...we own all this background material which really embodies Marvin's personality...Marvin has been superb. We have been like, "Can we show it to the kids and then the kids come up with a version as a performance?" and she was like, "Sure, do what you want with it!" Which was lovely. And Marvin's quite a charismatic person in that context; we got a particular patina to the presentation, very DIY, very enthusiasm-based. Now we have a massive archive of material that underpins the performance but has a life of its own as well.

It's really interesting. I was moderately anxious in doing a re-staging for Marvin, but fundamentally she knows the parameters. She understands that this isn't about highly skilled trained dance work. She is using dancers for displays of *Home Made Tasers* but she doesn't historically use dancers, she uses her own friends with their own enthusiasm. It's not about precise movement, it's performance art. The way it will be judged by an audience is not going to be on the quality of the physical representation. Matthias would never put me in that position. That's not something that I could fulfil, any more than I could conduct an orchestra.

But the challenge is that I'm a curator and it's fine that you kind of have to put a video on the wall but now I have to lead movement. I'm not a theatre director, but now I'm leading movement workshops with dancers! It's a real challenge. I'm going to end up asking for some mentoring because it's a really special set of skills. It's interesting that Marvin doesn't come from a theatre background, she comes from a visual arts background, but that role of the director is really accentuated within Marvin. It's the sort of thing she enjoys: putting a curator in this position where they have to lead movement workshops. But all of this is on video so we are also seeing her doing it – so it's been me leading via her role on video. It creates this really interesting dynamic. In this iteration we have some performers in Nottingham who work directly with her so we have a person-to-person transmission of information, which is something we'd like to sustain but can't quite guarantee. But the model we've got is that she is sending me these instructions, I get on with it and then she comes on the opening night and says, "This worked, that didn't." So I get a mark out of ten.

SW: Do you have previous experience of curating dance, and in this case, re-staging performance previously?

HW: It's not the arena that I historically worked in. I think this is one of the things that has come up...Catherine Wood has also discussed the changing role of the curator. I think beyond performance this idea of media-specific curating is already being seriously challenged. It doesn't make that much sense to talk about someone like Eddie Peake as either a performer or photographer or a filmmaker; he works across media, and that cross-media practice is pretty standard now. There are artists who only paint and do films but it's certainly an assumption that you can make. So the idea that curators have media-based specialisations is being eroded anyway. But the skill set required to curate or direct performance throws this experiential gap into stark relief.

The way you curate film has changed over time, the way you curate performance has changed over time. The example I like to use is Stuart Comer, who, when at Tate, talked about installing a Bruce Nauman piece, which was a 16mm film. They requested to transfer it to DVD, which Bruce Nauman said was fine; they could transfer it to DVD, which changes the visual quality of it, but then they had to add the soundtrack of the 16mm projector onto it. So visual quality of 16mm not part of artwork, clickety clackety sound constitutes artwork. This is kind of the meat of creating performance...you establish the parameters of what is required for the artwork to be present.

SW: What kind of contract do you typically have with dance and performance artists such as Matthias and Marvin?

HW: We talk a lot about contracts. The contract in some sense becomes the artwork. That is the document that becomes the script. With Matthias we talked about scores and how choreography is presented and documented. But within a visual arts form...the contract that we have with Marvin is a very standard acquisitions contract. But with the caveat that instructions must be followed, which is pretty open-ended. We've got instructions which are pretty open-ended, but there is also a lot of rigour in there.

What we were realising was that historically contracts are put into place to try and protect the institution, so that the other ten editions that are released don't devalue it or whatever. But in this context of performance, the reason that you have the contract in place is to ensure the integrity of the artwork on behalf of the artist in the future, and in my point of view, or from the institution's point of view, it's convenient for us to have a contract which says, "We have the artwork," and full stop. Because we can then, if we're short of money, have a few less performers in it, or we can change the lighting or whatever gives us a higher degree of flexibility, but it gives the possibility that we are quite likely not fulfilling the vision of the artist.

That was quite late on...that realisation...that understanding that the contract was there as a tool for the artist to use, more perhaps then the institution. What research are we doing in how we build a contract? They create problems for the institutions.

And really that's what it is about, this liveness: performers or artists coming into the building, into the collections and creating new works and new resonances in the space. Performance, at its best, rethinks the museum by unpicking the institution's archival instincts.

***Home Made Tasers* (2011)**
by Marvin Gaye Chetwynd
performers: Morgan Rournegoux,
Viniita Moran AKA Max Power,
Adam Christensen, Tamar Hirshfeld,
Vincent Guiomar & Marvin Gaye Chetwynd,
New Museum, New York,
26 October 2011–1 January 2012,
photo courtesy Marvin Gaye Chetwynd,
New Museum and Sadie Coles HQ

Matthias Sperling

Choreographer and Performer

SW: Could you begin by telling me about the work you made, *Effective Dance: healing procedure for a German Expressionist object,* for New Walk Museum and Art Gallery in Leicester?

MS: I could begin by telling you a little bit about the context of this piece, a project that was first performed in October last year, and one way of doing that is to tell you the information that I wrote for audience members to see. This was a new piece of work commissioned by New Walk and also supported a lot by Siobhan Davies Dance and Dance4. The text handed out to audience members said:

'Choreographer Matthias Sperling's new work attempts to intervene in the history of a German Expressionist art object by dancing at it. While seemingly absurd, the attempt is also a genuine one: Sperling engages with the object as having experienced a traumatic past, with particular reference to the Nazis' labelling of German Expressionist works as degenerate in 1937. His striving to effect a positive historical change through his movement becomes a way of questioning the apparent contrast between the ephemerality of action and the fixity of objects, and asking how our action in relation to artworks contributes to creating their identities.'

The way that this project began was that – I think Kate Coyne, Programme Director at Siobhan Davies Dance, met Hugo Worthy, the curator at New Walk – and Hugo mentioned that he was interested in commissioning a performance and wanted to talk to Kate and Siobhan Davies Dance about that. He was interested in commissioning something specifically in relation to a re-hang of the museum's collection of German Expressionist art. It's an incredible collection, actually the largest of its kind in the UK.

They did this re-hang, sort of a re-launch, of their display of the collection around the idea of the total artwork. I think Hugo was interested, in general, in working with performance in the museum and thought that this exhibition's focus on the total artwork was a really strong link with performance. And so the invitation at first was to make a tonal response to the exhibition, or alongside the exhibition, *Expressionism: The Total Artwork*, which is one room in this, I would say, medium-scale museum in Leicester. It's a municipal museum. Hugo was really open and he really welcomed that it could be anything that I wanted it to be. And that it didn't necessarily have to be an art historical response to this specific context of German Expressionism. That it could be something more tonally related. Tonal in the sense that it could have whatever kind of relationship I was interested in finding. So that was really wonderful.

SW: Tell me more about why that invitation from Hugo was of interest to you?

MS: One of the reasons why that invitation interested me was because of the specific context. I quickly learned that it was an extraordinary collection with a really amazing history. It's a really rich context to engage with.

I did loads of research. At first I was a bit worried that I didn't know that I was going to find a relationship between my practice and this exhibition context, but then in the course of research a lot of different possibilities emerged. As an example, some of the ways in which I found that German Expressionism was described in the texts I was looking at had resonance for me with things that I was already interested in. So, for instance, things like the emphasis on subjectivity in German Expressionism, I related to my interest in noticing that a performer is always an experiencing subject, and to my interest in noticing perception as an embodied act, as something that is always part of the unfolding of choreography, in both the performer and audience member. Also, the emphasis in German Expressionism on intuitive action, the unconscious, disinhibition of the unconscious, connected for me with my interest in the embodied intelligent unconscious – in considering how, like perception, the unconscious is an embodied process happening in performance and considering that one of the things that dance or live performance might offer is an opportunity to notice our negotiation with that embodied unconscious.

Then hypnosis links with that. I felt that a lot of the ways that German Expressionism is analysed in things I was reading reminded me of hypnosis in this kind of unleashing, re-patterning. And hypnosis is something I have been interested in looking at and working with. One of the strands of this project became working with a clinical psychologist who does hypnosis research at UCL, Dr. Val Walters, and experiencing hypnosis with her. In the session we made the subject of it the context of this performance. By that point, my ideas about the performance and this idea of healing the art object through my movement, were already pretty defined. So as she was talking me through this hypnosis session it was directly related to that scenario. Basically, I'm interested in thinking about how hypnosis might be an unusual way of describing embodied processes that are very usual in live performance and often integral to it. And one of the ways I think of my activity in this performance is as an attempt to perform a kind of hypnotherapeutic surgery on the object, by drawing on skills from my history of performance practice.

So in one sense there is this anthropomorphisation of the art object as a thing that has been around for a long time – the actual object I chose to direct my performance towards was made in 1921. So it has nearly a hundred years of history, of experience. Passing through various situations and places and then, at one point, under the Nazis it's all declared degenerate, and then later has this rehabilitation. What I was particularly interested in pointing towards was this idea that these apparently fixed objects do have mutable identities. And the thing that makes them mutable is people's actions towards them or people's engagement with them. I think of that, immediately, in terms of movement. How I move, including the movement of my perception in relation to this object, can – I hope or I propose – have some impact on its identity for me or, potentially, for others present. And what can we make of that, or with that?

SW: Can you talk more about the research that you did leading up to this work for New Walk?

MS: I consider the research that I did very much a part of the process of making the thing. And it was one of the ways in which I chose to use the commission budget, to put a lot of time in. Maybe it's interesting, also, to talk about the conditions in which this piece happened. Because I think this was, from my perspective, good practice. When Hugo approached – first Kate Coyne and Siobhan Davies Dance, and then through them, me – he already had in mind that he would earmark at least £5,000 for this commission. So immediately I thought, "OK, it's actually possible to do something for this amount of money and I can give a serious chunk of my time to making a serious piece of work." And then later on Siobhan Davies Dance offered a lot of in-kind support in terms of studio space and production support and marketing support, all sorts of things. And also Dance4 added in another £1,000 to the production budget when the needs of that production budget became more clear for me. That's partly through my relationship with Dance4 as an Associate Artist, and the museum being in their region as well.

SW: Who covered your travel expenses?

MS: I travelled there several times and it is not that expensive a journey. The commission fee was all inclusive. I should also say that Hugo and New Walk also added to the budget later on when we got more specific about documentation because we both decided we were really keen to have a proper video document of it, and we realised that the commission budget wouldn't stretch far enough to include that and the museum was able to draw on other funds to cover that for this project. So that added another £1,400 just for documentation. There was a really decent amount of support to work with.

SW: It sounds like you were able to facilitate supportive partnerships for the New Walk commission through your network and that these partners were the bridging elements which made the project possible.

MS: The bridging role that Siobhan Davies Dance played was really interesting. It's something that I am really fortunate to have because it is a middle ground between having a production structure and being an independent artist. And it's a really unique but really helpful balance that we had in this project and I think it's probably not something to think of as a permanent model but a moment in the trajectory of my collaboration with Siobhan Davies Dance and their support of me. I think that is very conscious on the part of Siobhan Davies Dance and on my part and it feels like a really essential process. A really genuine addressing of the current needs of artists in flexible ways. Also, specifically this dance organisation, Siobhan Davies Dance, has a lot of organisational experience of presenting performance in galleries, and in really practical things in terms of what to ask for and dressing room spaces to negotiate. A history of practice that becomes a support.

SW: Can you share the kinds of discussions you had with Hugo for this commission?

MS: Hugo and I had a lot of dialogue and that really supported me. I really enjoyed working with Hugo as a curator because he was really engaged with the process without making any demands on it that made me uncomfortable. I always felt supported and not limited by that engagement. As I gradually became clearer in my ideas then he was able to engage more specifically in feedback and that was helpful.

One thing that I really appreciated about Hugo's approach is he said, "I have never done this before, I am really happy to learn. As an organisation this museum has never done this before. We are going to make some mistakes." He's very interested in learning on lots of levels, also in terms of his conceptual engagement, in learning more about the different histories alongside the practicalities.

SW: It sounds like there was a close and collaborative relationship during your process. How were decisions taken regarding the presentation of the work?

MS: Hugo asked that the result of this commission be performed at the opening on two evenings. Then, beyond that, it could be performed other times. It could have any duration or form that I chose. What I chose, partly because of the time scale and budget, was for it to be performed specifically during the openings and not other times. The context is of an exhibition opening with many invited people. The first night was invited guests and the second night was a public opening. I conceived the performance as only occurring in the gallery when there was a substantial audience gathered there as part of an event.

SW: How would you define your work within that context and, more precisely, in relationship to a specific artwork in the gallery?

MS: I see what I made as an artwork. When I make dances I am attempting to make artworks. I consider dance as one form within the larger category of art, and I find it more possible to think about the relationship that what I make might have with the rest of the world when I focus on those kinds of larger categories. So I see what I made as a work and it is specific and can be performed again in other times and places. I like the way that Hugo articulated it once, "It's a performance that is art historically situated." So it's positioned in relation to German Expressionism as an art historical period. And it can travel in time and space but always needs to find this orientation with this art historical referent. I really love the idea that within that scenario, which includes an art historical object and a live performance, that there is potential for reversals in the relationship between what is fixed and what is mutable. That perhaps the object, the identity of the object, is mutable, while the procedure of the performance remains fixed.

SW: This all sounds very positive. I am wondering if there is anything that, in retrospect, you would have done differently or wished for?

MS: One thing that emerged, on the night of the first performances, was that we realised something we hadn't thought to talk about before. It was the presence of TV cameras and press photographers in the room that I didn't expect to be there. So it was a question of communication between me and the museum, and not just me and the curator, but the marketing department of the museum. Because the marketing department, obviously, had a responsibility to arrange how the event would be documented and disseminated beyond the museum. What we hadn't quite joined up is that things like a local television news camera with a bright light on it alters the situation that I have intended for this performance, and press photographers with shutters clicking away also alter the atmosphere of a mostly quiet performance. We can arrange an appropriate time for that photography to happen. It can be done in ways that are sensitive to a particular event if there is time to develop a sense of what that is. We suddenly realised we hadn't done that, and I needed to ask them – just before beginning the performance – to not document, because we had already invested in producing appropriate documentation that was embedded in my understanding of the whole event. There were certain positive results, because one press photographer who refused to stop taking pictures took some nice images. It was fine, but it was a conversation that we realised that it would have been better to have had previously.

SW: Can you speak about your work in relationship to its audience, the visitors in the gallery who come to see your work?

MS: What I am interested in is the judgement of effectiveness being made by the people who are present, including me as a performer and the audience. I think I am really interested in both myself and audience members consciously engaging in a process of judging effectiveness during the performance.

SW: Are you suggesting, then, that the audience in the gallery offers a form of feedback for your work?

MS: I think there are lots of forms of feedback and some of them are in the moment of performance. In my perception of audience members' responses and audience members' ways of engaging with the performance in the moment it is happening, and also in things that people mentioned afterwards, the ways that people behaved. After I left the room and the performance finished, some people went up to scrutinise in detail the object that I had just been dancing at. And we had a more organised public talk that audience members could contribute to as well. But I think what interests me the most is this subjective and intuitive judgement of effectiveness on each person's part.

SW: Going back to the text that you read to me in the beginning of our talk and that was made available for the audience members before seeing your work; what was important to you about that text and/or why you felt a need to share that information with your audience prior to them seeing the work?

MS: It was important for me to have the text and I felt that I really wanted people to know the title because, for me, the title is always part of the work and it gives information. And I really wanted people to know what I was working on, also because this was one of the first times this museum was presenting a commissioned performance work, and I wanted to make sure people had a way in. One of the things that I often play with is the simultaneousness of seriousness and non-seriousness in what I am doing. And sometimes I feel that I need to signal that to people because audience members can assume it must be prohibited to acknowledge the absurdity of what I am doing. When, in fact, what I am doing is inviting them to acknowledge that, as well as see my genuine engagement. It was just about giving permission in a way. I think people can see what I am doing but not why.

SW: Do you think that dance in the gallery or museum space – and in relationship to the field of the visual arts – allows for certain exchanges?

MS: My view is that dance in museums is part of the field, not outside of the field, of what I am doing; to do choreography in a museum as one of the potential places where it might happen. I am speaking from a perspective where, in the last few years, almost everything that I'm doing is in the context of a gallery or a museum. It was interesting going through the process of choosing one project to speak about today because it made me realise, in fact, there are more than 20 projects, or 20 occasions of working in galleries or museums, that I could talk about. Some of that is from doing the same work in different places, but that is actually now what I do most often. I definitely have remained enthusiastic about that, but at the same time I haven't explicitly made a conscious choice to stop spending time on a theatre stage or making work for that context. In fact, I tend to find it more possible to explore the things I want to explore in the gallery or museum context.

***Effective Dance: healing procedure for a German Expressionist object* (2014) by Matthias Sperling,**
performer: Matthias Sperling,
New Walk Museum and Art Gallery, Leicester,
3 October 2014,
photo by Neil Wissink

Katye Coe

Dance Artist

SW: Can you talk about your work as a dance maker, and your experience as one of the curated dance artists in *Volumes Project* – the live performance component of *MIRRORCITY* at Hayward Gallery?

KC: I feel that I am perhaps less experienced than many in receiving invitations to show my own work. My work as a maker is becoming visible only more recently and in particular in relation to larger institutions. I have, however, been inside invitations with a role as a performer in projects over many years, and have also curated for almost a decade in different spaces and contexts. The Hayward exhibition operated as an unusual invitation to practise an already conceived work, *(to) constantly vent*, over twelve weeks.

I can also offer maybe a broader response from my own navigation of being in *Volumes Project*. It remains, historically, quite rare to have a group of dance works invited as artworks inside a gallery group show or exhibition and over a long period of time. *(to) constantly vent* also had a life over three days in Stockholm at *The Dancer as Agent* conference in November 2013. This piece of work hasn't actually ever had a life in the theatre. The closest it got to a theatre setting was at *what_now 2013*, its original commission. Frank Bock curated it as one of a series of events, some of which were performance and many of which were not. *(to) constantly vent* doesn't propose itself really as a theatrical intervention, making it perhaps distinct from the other works shown in *Volumes Project* at Hayward and also in its previous performance situations. In all these situations, spectators were coming to experience complete works, objects or things that had a start and finish.

SW: How did being in the Hayward – and in relation to that same work of yours having been shown in other venues – meet the requirements of that work and/or your practice?

KC: Many gallery spaces operate as a space that cannot always meet all the theatrical requirements of a piece of movement practice or a dance work due to the architecture or resources of an institution. It is strange to make demands on such a structure, and yet necessary for us as dance practitioners to find solutions to the problem of concrete floors, lack of studio space, differences in lighting.

(to) constantly vent has a particular set of complications. For example, the principle technical requirement of the work is that the sound of the running is heard live and constantly throughout the time that it's occurring. There should be a live phone line linked to wireless speakers, meaning that when the movement is not visible, which is for a great deal of the time, people in the gallery space or theatre or conference space can always hear the activity of the running whether they can see it or not. Hayward is a concrete building and therefore mobile phone reception is an issue and live linked sound was not available. We had to let go of one of the fundamental parts of the work then, fairly early in the process, and rethink or reconstruct its sound. I had not encountered before the complex nature of the install for a huge group show, and found myself in the midst of huge numbers of technicians and production and curatorial staff. The attention that they had to pay to all the works being installed was all-encompassing, and I found that my usual technical and production expectations needed to adjust to a different structure.

I think it is easy to forget that we always have a choice in these types of circumstance. I could say, "Yes, I continue and I work with these compromises," or I could say, "No, I can't realise my work so I won't show my work." I chose the former.

SW: In the running through the space that exists in this work, did you have any issues in relation to the other artworks in the gallery?

KC: *(to) constantly vent* saw the performers running continual circuits through the gallery space. The health and safety team there did a very thorough witness of the work and we were given a route that was at the core of the building and yet peripheral to most of the artworks, and vulnerable or fragile works were avoided. The runner passed along the main runways in the building where people might walk as they're going from one level to another. We ran in through the foyer and past the ticket desk, upslope, through the back of the gallery, up the stairs, along the white wall, back downstairs and out through the shop.

Frank Bock described it as a particular kind of 'retinal seeing or experience'. It wasn't sitting or being amongst the other artworks for anything beyond a split-second. There was no direct intervention with the artworks themselves, certainly no danger of any damage, and the intervention of the work in that way could remain much more obtuse in its relationship to the other works.

SW: We all know that one is not supposed to run in the museum. I am curious about the invisible or not-so-invisible social codes of behaviour in the museum and how your work might have intervened in those.

KC: People pay particular attention to the exhibits in a gallery, in a museum, and the running body doesn't do that. It doesn't have the time to pay the attention that is coded as appropriate for a gallery or a museum setting. That was very liberating for us as performers and, hopefully, also for the attention of the person watching. You know, you stand and you look at a sculpture, or you stand and you watch a body. What *(to) constantly vent* intends is that you don't stand and you don't watch. You see something pass you and that is the experience of it. You may hear something over time, but you may or may not associate that with the activity of the body in the gallery space.

The other thing worth noting is the relationship *Volumes Project* built up with the other bodies and communities in and around the gallery space. One of these groups was the gallery invigilators. The life of the invigilators as they attend the works is similar to the marking of time that happens when you perform through a space over many days and weeks. Here is a set of people or workers who spend an enormous amount of time in more or less the same place over hours; who also in some way mirror the exhibits. It was a really interesting process for us to navigate the economies and the hierarchies of the gallery, and of the people who work inside of the museum space, and that they were entirely different in how they chose to or chose not to relate to the practices we brought in.

SW: On the subject of human bodies (and in the case of *(to) constantly vent*), can you talk about the conditions of this piece and how you took care of the runners/performers within the gallery?

KC: There is a very particular set of conditions that happen when the body runs over many hours. I was probably quite hyperaware of that when I went in, because I'm a runner and so I know what it is to run. I chose to work with people that run as part of their practice. They (Hetty Blades, Taylan Halici, Hannah McBrien and Jamila Rodrigues) were performers that were skilled as runners. No one got injured over the course of the exhibition.

One of the major advantages that I found working with and having the recorded sound was that we could actually pause. We could go to the toilet, take breaks and stop running, momentarily, when the running was not visible. When you have live sound going on, the real constant rhythm of the running is imperative. It would have been a different story if we'd had the live sound running because we'd have had to have more people and I think that the bodies would have experienced a different level of fatigue.

SW: Do you think the gallery or museum space might be more suitable for running as a movement, and for *(to) constantly vent*, than a proscenium theatre space?

KC: I make work and am involved in work that is, in essence, always evolving. The running has a set of conditions that has demands; it has to make a circuit through the space; it has to come in through one door and leave through another door; it has to be continuous. So there are spaces for which it wouldn't work, but there are many spaces and situations in which it could, and has existed.

SW: Your practice moves across different spatial and contextual platforms. Does the spatial context drive the way that you work or what you make?

KC: I think that if the space can, in some way, provide a light on the practice then I am not necessarily, unless invited to, making work for a specific kind of space, or a space that has a particular set of rules or conventions. A flexibility of thinking inside the frame of making comes from a way that the practice often arrives in and from multiple situations. I imagine that when I'm performing in other people's practices or performances, I am still practising creatively; it's just in a different frame. It's been helpful for me not to position myself as a choreographer or director or performer. There's just one body of practice that reveals itself in different ways.

What we as artists need to do is get on with making and performing the work, and allow the context and the frame of it to be part of that process, but not necessarily, unless it's our curiosity, to be so bound up with how it's received and where it's received. I don't know, it might be a red herring, but I feel there's something in that that sometimes trips us up. The proposition is that the dancing is seen for nothing and so the exchange at the moment of encounter is different. It could only be seen as fleeting and a moment of a body passing through space. When we set up the body to be seen, we are setting up a frame where the people watching the bodies, and the bodies themselves being watched, bring a particular set of overwhelming responsibilities on both sides, and I think we get stuck.

How we invite being seen, how we invite our work to be seen, how the body is being seen, how we deal with the performing body and how we deal with the different lenses that we place on that, from a feminist perspective to an analytical lens...I think that there is something that's very related to care in gallery spaces and perhaps the all-too-easy ignoring of the problems of the theatre. Maybe what's come up for me in the making or the realisation of my practice is the comparison to a totally conventional theatre space. We can become overwhelmed with responsibility in relation to how something is seen. I think we get stuck, and the gallery can magnify that, and can also negate it. People are able to pass by or through a performance in ways that they're not allowed to in a theatre space.

***(to) constantly vent* (2014)**
by Katye Coe
performer: Katye Coe,
part of *MIRRORCITY: London artists on fiction and reality*, Hayward Gallery, London,
13 October 2014–4 January 2015,
photo by Michael Brzezinski

EXHIBITION
CONTINUES

Joe Moran

Choreographer and Artistic Director,
Dance Art Foundation

SW: I have prompted you to talk about dance in gallery and museum spaces; where would you like to start?

JM: I am interested in the gallery and the museum to a degree. I am more interested, increasingly, in a third space. The opportunity of something like Tate Tanks, even though it's housed in a museum. Project spaces, or more flexible spaces, like at Nottingham Contemporary or the spaces at Tramway in Glasgow, interest me greatly. Spaces which are less codified by theatre or by the gallery. I think Nottingham Contemporary space works very successfully in that way; very much an in-between space. The gallery operates differently to the project space in what is shown and how it relates to the curatorial programme, so it is seen as other to the gallery. I feel it's less about dance being invited into the gallery, rather choreographing artists' films, and collaborating with individual artists.

My hope is for a space with greater potential, that somehow sits between the gallery and the theatre. That disrupts both those canons and complicates them. So rather than dance as an occupant in a gallery or a sculptural object in the gallery, or dance in a theatre or viewed in a theatrical frame, we may conflate those canons in perhaps quite an interesting way and we may be less restricted.

I curated a show at The Place, *Differ and Repeat* (2011). The concern of the show was choreography as a form, subject and discipline that may be distinct from dance and dancing. It was a kind of survey of artists' work, with a very strong curatorial focus, which, for me, speaks to an interest about curation as a choreographic practice. In this case, in terms of spatial and temporal concerns across a building. It operated as a choreography, as a kind of meta-choreography. It was very categorically not an exhibition. It wasn't presented in a visual arts space, it wasn't presented in a theatre. It was presented in an arts centre; in a dance centre but not located in a theatre. It was located in studios and spaces. That was a very definitive interest or choice of mine. I wasn't seeking a kind of visual art curatorial enquiry. It was a curatorial enquiry around performance rather than necessarily sitting in a visual arts reference. That then leads us to an enquiry about curation and where curation as an idea is located and why it's so often considered to be a visual art practice. I think we can have curation in dance and performance; I'm very interested in that, and it doesn't need to be located in a visual art context. I think there's an increasing discourse around the idea of curation in the digital space, but especially in dance there is a kind of tension between programming and curating.

SW: Traditionally, in certain contexts we call it 'programming', not 'curation' in dance. What do you think the difference might be between programming work and curating work?

JM: I'm not necessarily sure about the difference between programming and curating; it is something to do with the degree of artistic engagement in the development or conception of the work. Curatorially, I may bring together different works within an artistic vision, which I appreciate we could say is what a programmer does. I think, in general, festivals feel more curated to me than dance or a kind of ongoing theatre programme, which feels like a very different proposition.

I do think it is an exciting time for dance in the gallery, about which there has obviously been a huge amount, as we know, discussed or written already. In this moment, I am not entirely sure where we have arrived at. As an art form, we have really learned through hundreds of years of experience the conditions that are needed for a live event. A lot of it has to do with time and organisation of time. Dance, as an art form – and theatre more widely – has profound knowledge that it can share with other art forms, and I think that's fantastic.

SW: Is there an example where you worked in a gallery or museum that could be considered a best practice or that really worked for you?

JM: I did a show at Wilkinson Gallery in 2008. They had just moved into the very extraordinary, large space on Vyner Street. There was great collaboration around the marketing of the show. It was a curious show because we were constructing a theatre, to some degree, within the gallery. There was a lot of support for the show. They de-installed an entire gallery for the one night. It was an empty space. I had the whole gallery upstairs for a warm up space, which was closed. It was huge. I felt very taken care of. Also I was doing a solo, performing myself. That was very positive, the kind of very simple things. I installed a film work in the foyer so it was a diptych of the film installation and the solo which was time based. It was in the evening as well, so it wasn't really using the gallery during gallery hours.

SW: I am curious about your most recent work. Can you talk, in particular, about the title and how that might relate to some of the things we are discussing here?

JM: My current project is called *Why Everyone Wants What We've Got* and I'm currently subtitling it *Why Have I Bitten Off More Than I Can Chew?*. The project is changing very swiftly. It was conceived in response to two things: one, I did a talk at the Southbank Centre for the biennial symposium *The School of Sound.* It was the first time they'd invited a dance artist to contribute to the festival. It is an extraordinary international gathering of individuals who work with sound. I presented on the relationship between dance and music, or movement and sound. I offered a highly subjective historical lecture-performance on, in a way, the evolution of the relationship. From classical to modern to contemporary to postmodern dance. It was very wide ranging. I invited some dancers to perform with me and we created performance live. Lots of people came to me and said, "I had no idea there was so much thinking in dance." I felt very inspired by that, and very excited to be in that conversation. What do we know and how do we make that accessible or, rather, knowable?

That coupled with the experience of taking part in a *Dance and Art Forum* at Siobhan Davies Studios. One central question that arose was: what does the museum want from dance? We need to work that out. I felt a lot of what was said was very important and asking questions that dance needs to ask. I was talking about, historically, dance being economically deprived... the lowly relation...economically and critically judged as a lower art form. There is a reality institutionally, not just in terms of scale, but in terms of critical knowledge. We have a younger history of art – if we don't connect to ballet – if we're thinking about contemporary dance. If we think about the politics of subjugation, you have the dominant power who dictates or determines ideology, and then you have the disadvantaged other. In a way I think that has been the relationship between the visual arts and dance. So we ask the question: how then is dance using the visual arts; or how is dance changing that environment?

Those experiences inspired *Why Everyone Wants What We've Got*, and, increasingly, I'm not interested in a negative discourse or being in negative relation to the visual arts. Actually I work loads in the visual arts, and it really excites me. I think what I want to do with that project is to really...in the spirit of the Southbank talk...speak up for dance and, in a way, communicate to those fascinated by dance some of my very subjective opinions about why I think dance is extraordinary; why there is this endemic, unparalleled fascination with dance, in philosophy, in visual arts, in mass media, at this moment.

> **SW:** You make the choice to say (in your title), *Why Everyone Wants What We've Got*. As you are speaking, I am thinking about your subtitle: *Why I've Bitten Off More Than I Can Chew*. Can you speak more about that? Can you talk about your choice of viewpoint? In terms of it prompting dancers to look at themselves and what they have, versus looking outside of dance and what is out there that dance wants.

JM: Absolutely. What has changed over the last years? I think the Yvonne Rainer performances last summer, *Yvonne Rainer: Dance Works* at Raven Row, were a game changer. I don't quite know why. I haven't arrived at that yet. It just felt very clear that there was this real excitement in the visual arts and gallery for live work. I feel a kind of cynicism and suspicion lifting. On the back of that, and what I'm very keen to shift into, is a position where we own that. So that we own that it doesn't have to be a fight; we could perhaps own that people love what we do. There's a real excitement for what we do, and we've got something really, really remarkable.

I don't want to be inauthentically positive, but I want to have a different paradigm and I think it is possible. In a way that, for me, going round the houses with this, the energy in the title, that kind of spirited sense of saying, "We're fantastic, and everyone wants some of it." And so they should, because dance is extraordinary. We have the ability to speak up for that and to take that into the world. I don't mean that in an instrumentalist way or in a sense that our work is this all-fantastic thing. A lot of dance is enormously helpful in its agitation, or its pessimism, or its failure.

The subtitle is a joke. It just feels like...if we're thinking institutionally, it's so easy, I think, to fuck people off. I'm not shying away from that. I have a very good friend who's an actor, he has been an actor for twenty years. His knowledge of interpersonal dynamics, power plays and power struggles and the needs of the artist is profound. When I want to talk about something difficult that is happening with a group of students or a group of artists and I want to unpack that, he is this incredible body of knowledge. He talks passionately about the risk of making work. What it means to personally, artistically, critically put ourselves on the line in being an artist and being a performer. The degree of personal risk that's involved.

So coming back to the subtitle, *Why I've Bitten Off More Than I Can Chew*, in a way I'm frightened by this as a project. What am I getting myself into? I think it's so easy to attack the gallery, to attack the visual art curator, in a way that demeans. There's a lot of writing that I've been reading; the articles by artists for the Movement Research *Critical Correspondence* blog that includes contributions on dance in the museum and some of them are very critical.

I feel that the risk of the artist is also the risk of the curator to say, "This really excites me. Maybe I don't have the extent of the knowledge that the choreographer does – or maybe I do." Many curators, of course, have an extraordinary knowledge of performance, but of course in many cases their knowledge is of performance art, not of dance. Boris Charmatz famously reflected that history of the body in performance art can negate the entire history of falling, for example, as we know it in contemporary and modern dance. There can be whole articles in art theory about falling as if it's never been engaged with in dance as an idea. I also don't want to shut dialogue down. This project is conceived in the spirit of agitational confrontation, but hopefully fruitful. I've in fact changed my perspective greatly since starting this project, which was my hope as I learn and think more, and I feel very grateful for that.

SW: It is a great ambition, your championing of dance.

JM: Of course dance is concerned with the body. Around which there is already so much anxiety, of wanting to subjugate the body, to silence it, to ridicule it, to police it. Dance has been so complicit. We've been so willing in that. In many ways I am grateful to have pursued a less conventional or more independent training, allowing me to not be quite so complicit. But of course I'm just as much the good little dancer who will give the choreographer intuitively what they want without asking. Disciplined pleasers, really.

SW: Where will you present your new work, as I assume the choice of spaces is important to you and your work?

JM: I am working on a new collaboration I am exploring with a sculptor, Eva Rothschild, for which I am thinking about those third spaces. I am excited about that project because it feels very much about the meeting of our compositional interests in different forms; a collaborative performance project that will bring together those interests. We have developed a kind of manifesto for what our principles or values are for what we want to pursue. It concerns the material or materiality of the body, the dancer, the material of the object, and how they meet or don't meet.

Eva has described that at times she can envy the theatrical audience, the rapt, obedient audience (maybe emancipated, hopefully); an audience that doesn't just walk by, but who gives attention willingly and signs up to something. That is something we have that I don't think we always value. In dance, we often pursue a different intimacy to the theatrical; we want a different temporal experience where people come and go. But for many artists that feels very...OK, of course there's the agency of the spectator... but it can also be very dishonouring maybe, or there's not a lot of care and attentiveness given. The journey of being in an audience where you are there, where it may even be a gruelling experience where you're actually challenged in your patience and your boredom and your generosity to meet the work. It is a fascinating idea.

For the lecture performance, I think I will take it into galleries. That piece feels like it could just be in a lecture hall, probably also universities. I don't quite know where it's going to end up, but I feel it very definitely needs to be performative as well as a lecture. I did a presentation recently for an interview. I like taking the time to try to communicate very simply about my work, in a way that is not dense and not academically referenced. So maybe it might go in that direction.

I think there's a tension around, for me, in this project, the tension of dance and theory.

I have talked a lot about spaces and I think we need new spaces for dance. I think we need project spaces. I would really love Dance Art Foundation to have a project space – like at Nottingham Contemporary – which is a curated space for research, sharing and conversation like Weld in Stockholm. It's not really about performance – they don't really have a programme, but they do performance; it's kind of an amazing research context, a social context. I think that we need that.

***Maesk* (2014)**
by Joe Moran
performers: Samuel Kennedy,
Dominick Mitchell-Bennett, Erik Nevin,
Christopher Owen, Alex Standard,
Yiannis Tsigkris,
An Evening of Performances,
David Roberts Art Foundation, London,
16 October 2014,
photo by Josh Redman

Stephanie Rosenthal

Chief Curator,
Hayward Gallery

SW: As a way to start, I would like to invite you to speak about your approach to curating dance at Hayward Gallery.

SR: My main approach is to say, "If I integrate dance or choreography in my shows, it has to be as present as a painting or a sculpture." I realise, however, that's a really difficult task because Hayward shows usually run for three or four months and are open 8 hours a day. Most dance is presented for five days or so. When it comes to dance there are a lot of reasons why most choreographies do not run for months and do not have a duration of eight hours. On the other hand, if you integrate dance into the museum for shorter periods, it is separated because it's not part of the large exhibition. So there are a lot of pragmatic things which are not solved yet because dance in galleries is not something that continuously happens.

SW: What do you mean precisely?

SR: I mean precisely three things: budget, concept and availability. First, I think a lot about budget implications and how difficult it actually is to do things in a correct way, such as paying people enough, treating the performers like artists. If you put up a large exhibition, the justification for putting a budget of half a million in is that you run it for three months with the benefit being that people get to see it for a longer time. However, costs are more or less 'closed' once the exhibits have arrived and are displayed in the museum. If you do the same thing with a dance piece, it means that every day you are accumulating more expense; you need a budget for the stage manager, the lighting manager, the dancers. It always goes back to needing a huge budget to do it really right, or it goes back to these small projects which can almost disappear in the gallery. Also, apart from budgets, availability is a problem. Dance artists all have other rehearsals, so they can't necessarily say that they can be available for three months. At the moment I am curating the Sydney Biennale, where I would like to include a lot of performance and dance, and I am precisely faced with these two problems – budget and the fact that there is no contemporary dance in Australia. So I would have to fly in the dancers – again: budget! Those are the struggles that I still have because I feel that the most interesting thing for me is the encounter that the audience has when experiencing dance which does not have a start and an end time, but to come across the movement like you do with a sculpture or a painting. To have that kind of presence in a space means you need a lot of performers; most of the time a lot of skilled performers.

SW: That is probably the question of concept. It sounds like you prefer having durational dance works because it helps to integrate them into the exhibition, is that correct?

SR: Yes, if dance is the integral part of an exhibition that I'm doing, how could I accept that a part is suddenly missing for six hours a day? If you think of an art show as a piece of choreography where every element plays an important role, then it's quite difficult to say that parts are missing sometimes. It's like doing a play saying: "50% of the time, Act III doesn't exist." Therefore it's difficult for me as a curator if I don't consider it as an essential or integral part. If you don't consider it, it becomes the little thing aside which is nice to have. That doesn't mean that you can't say, "I'm having a programme of performances related to an exhibition and it just unfolds over time," and presuming someone has the time to come to everything. Then you have a parallel programme. But that is not so much my interest in bringing dance into the museum. I'm more interested in that form that says that these pieces are either commissioned, so born in and for an exhibition, or they have a tradition of being done in that form.

There are, of course, so many other varieties of what you could do. The Tate does have performance spaces. They have now taken the next step and have the Tanks. Then again, it is a stage, it's not an exhibition. I don't think it's a step back; I think it's a step in a direction, maybe, that is necessary. Otherwise we might not be able to integrate dance in collections. I think we are in a time now where we have to think more, because there are so many different forms of dance in the museum.

SW: Are you suggesting that the way forward is for galleries and museums to provide proper performance and/or theatre spaces for dance?

SR: I am basically trying to make the point that to have a stage or a dedicated obvious platform for dance/performance is one way to go.

SW: How would having a dedicated dance space affect your interest in durational works at Hayward?

SR: For a place like Hayward, where we have changing exhibitions and not a collection, it's not so relevant to have the pieces, the staged or space-defined timed pieces. It's not really what we are doing. Others, like Walker Art Center in Minneapolis, do present dance on a stage. I think that's very relevant.

SW: In staying with the discussion of durational works, can you speak to the time demand that such an approach might place on the dancers, as well as on the gallery staff?

SR: It's about scheduling and what the pieces are. I don't think we will ever be at the point where the dancer wants to dance for eight hours on concrete. If you do a durational piece over eight hours, of course it's not necessarily eight hours of dancing. If you think about the dance pieces, or the choreographic works that are put into museums, they are rarely ever straining like Yvonne Rainer's *Trio A*. That's probably also something I learned from the exhibition *Move: Choreographing You*; that *Trio A* wasn't meant to be in a museum durationally. You really have to have a quite elaborate schedule saying how long you can do something, and it depends on the pieces. For example, Xavier Le Roy would always make durational pieces that take into consideration what's acceptable for a dancer and in what way can that be done.

SW: As part of your exhibition *MIRRORCITY*, that showed works of London-based artists who explored the challenges, conditions and consequences of living in a digital age, you programmed a series of performances that focused on the physical body as a means of exploring actual space. You brought in Frank Bock, Nicola Conibere and Martin Hargreaves to take on the selection of dance artists. I am curious if you considered the performances as a component of *MIRRORCITY* or as a curated project within a curated project?

SR: *Volumes Project* came in and then developed. I invited Frank, Nicola and

Martin as a collective. They are artists, and they decided that they wanted to invite other artists. In my world you would say, "Well, you invited a group of artists and that's their work," but in this case I think it was something else. I don't think Martin, Frank or Nicola would say that it was their work. I think they would really say, "This is the work of different people that we curated." So it was a project in a project, out of necessity.

SW: Can you talk about your involvement with *Volumes Project* in terms of communication with Nicola, Frank and Martin?

SR: Initially I was very involved, actually giving them quite a clear idea of what I wanted from the invited artists and what I would want from the piece. They did something quite different, but I think it worked much better than what I had wanted. It was one of those examples where I thought, "Because I have given so much over, it actually worked much better." Sometimes you just have to say, "They're great, just trust."

SW: In what ways did they do things, as you said, 'differently'?

SR: The artists that Frank, Nicola and Martin selected made pieces that were much less process-oriented. I was interested in inviting artists to explore the space during the run of the show. But I understood 'exploring the space' in a much more literal way. I wanted to have artists develop the piece with the audience over the run of the three months. What Frank, Nicola and Martin did, and what worked really well, was that they picked pieces which were very sculptural. From my perspective, and I think they would disagree a bit, I thought they were highly conservative and picked something quite safe. But then I think by doing that, they really made the experience of the visitor much more relevant for opening these doors to having dance in the museum. With these pieces in *Volumes Project*, people would say, "Oh, did you see this?" And they would try to come back and see another one. Whereas, for example, in *Move: Choreographing You* hardly anyone mentioned Xavier Le Roy and Mårten Spångberg's piece, which was really important to me, but it was much more subtle and invisible.

SW: And how were things communicated for *Volumes Project* with your staff, in particular the invigilators, in terms of what was happening in the space and interaction with the visitors?

SR: It's quite an interesting question. The invigilators have the responsibility of protecting the work, which is difficult without being clear about what is needed, and causes frustration. I learned this from *Move*; how to explain that sometimes a dancer is very vulnerable, so you need an invigilator who's, in a subtle way, taking care so you know nothing is happening. If someone is in a vulnerable static position, people start to touch, and there can be unpleasant situations. You're not secure like you are on a stage; you're in the inner space with other people. What we did with *Volumes Project* was much easier for our security guards than the *Move* exhibition, because it was more defined in space and time.

SW: I am remembering your comment earlier about your assumption or expectation that the artists in *Volumes Project* would work more in the spaces of Hayward leading up to the show itself. Why do you think that did not happen in the way you might have imagined?

SR: The *Volumes Project* artists often came down to very pragmatic decisions. They said, "There's not a lot of time. We don't have a huge budget." They obviously knew what they were doing. They're professional. They wanted to do it right. So better to pick pieces which exist and then develop in the space, rather than developing a piece in the space. The dance artists know that they are vulnerable when they are developing something and maybe did not want to do it in that context. Also Hayward Gallery – and there is another point when it comes to dance and galleries – is in many ways crazy for dancers. If we have dancers and musicians in the Royal Festival Hall, they get their own room, their own drinks; they get some food; they have bathrooms. If you walk into the Hayward Gallery you have to change in the toilets probably. So for *Volumes Project* we built a space for the dancers and their needs.

What Martin said when we had our debrief was that, during the run of the show, he realised that he needed a stage manager. I remember with *Move* this was totally new for me, and after the first month of research I realised that if you have dance, the floor has to be sprung...I was totally naïve about certain things. If you think about it, of course no one can dance on a concrete floor every day for two hours. You can severely injure yourself. It's true that we had never really thought about it in this way, but you need a coordinator, which we had for *Move*. It's not just running; it's communicating and working with the needs of the dance artist.

> **SW:** It references the needs of artworks to be stored when they are not on display; that care-taking for the artwork or, in the case of dance, the physical body is important.

SR: This is what we're still learning. I remember we had Siobhan Davies Dance, I think three years ago, and we talked a lot about the practical aspects of working in a space. I think that's a movement now, because probably people like Catherine Wood, myself, Turner Contemporary; we are becoming aware.

> **SW:** Do you have any sense of how dance in the gallery and museum might be taken care of or further supported in the future?

SR: I do think museums will go more in the direction of having a stage, as we spoke about earlier. But I think the way it is happening in the Tate is creating, not an extremely theatrical space, but one where dance can happen in a defined area. I think there are new possibilities. You can present dance for the whole day; kind of open up what feels like an exhibition space and a performance space. Approaches towards dance in museums are changing constantly, because the more you do, the more you learn – this works; this doesn't work; this is interesting; this is not interesting.

***Swell the thickening surface of* (2013)**
by Florence Peake
performer: Hamish MacPherson,
part of *MIRRORCITY, London artists on fiction and reality*, Hayward Gallery, London,
13 October 2014–4 January 2015,
photo by Michael Brzezinski.

Florence Peake would like to give acknowledgement to all the dancers who took part in this performance: Gaby Agis, Luke Birch, Neil Brown, Rachel Gildea, Lizzy Le Quesne, Catherine Long, Hamish MacPherson, Nando Messias, Joe Moran, Amaara Raheem, Carolyn Roy, Nikki Tomlinson and Rosalie Wahlfrid.

Images

TIM
ETCH

cK

p138–139
***If Tate Modern was Musée de la danse?* (2015)**
by Boris Charmatz
Tate Modern, London,
15 & 16 May 2015,
photo by Hugo Glendinning

p140–141
***The Pedestrians* (2011)**
by Charles Atlas
Mika Tajima and New Humans
event choreographed
by Gaby Agis
South London Gallery, London,
1–21 April 2011,
photo by Mike Blower

p142–143
***I am a Robot* (2014)**
by Charlie Morrissey
performer: Charlie Morrissey,
part of *MIRRORCITY: London artists on fiction and reality*,
Hayward Gallery, London,
13 October 2014–4 January 2015,
photo by Michael Brzezinski

p144–145
***Effective Dance: healing procedure for a German Expressionist object* (2014)**
by Matthias Sperling
performer: Matthias Sperling,
New Walk Museum and Art Gallery,
Leicester, 3 October 2014,
photo by Neil Wissink

p146–147
***Diagonal* (part of *Terrain*) (1963)**
by Yvonne Rainer
performed by Povilas Bastys,
Irina Baldini, Rosalie Wahlfrid,
Alice MacKenzie, Samuel Kennedy,
Sara Wookey, Emilia Gasiorek,
Morrighan MacGillivray & Antigone Avdi,
part of *Yvonne Rainer: Dance Works*,
Raven Row, London,
11 July–10 August 2014,
photo by Eva Herzog

p148–149
***Do-Re-Me* (2014)**
by Nicola Conibere
performers: Neil Callaghan
& Ben McEwen,
part of *MIRRORCITY: London artists on fiction and reality*,
Hayward Gallery, London,
13 October 2014–4 January 2015

p150–151
***YARD 1961/2014* (2014)**
by Allan Kaprow
performance intervention
by Janine Harrington
performer: Elisa Vassena
The Calder at The Hepworth
Wakefield, Wakefield,
4 July–31 August 2014,
photo by Tom Arber,
courtesy of The Hepworth Wakefield

p152–153
***To hand* (2011)**
by Siobhan Davies in collaboration with Matthias Sperling
performer: Matthias Sperling,
Whitechapel Gallery, London,
2–20 March 2011,
photo by Pari Naderi

p154–155
***Lecture from The Mind Is a Muscle* (1968)**
by Yvonne Rainer
Yvonne Rainer performs *Trio A*
in tap shoes while Gay Delanghe,
Steve Paxton, Becky Arnold and
Barbara Dilley observe,
Anderson Theatre, New York,
photo by Peter Moore

p156–157
***YARD 1961/2014* (2014)**
by Allan Kaprow
installation view, The Calder at
The Hepworth Wakefield, Wakefield,
4 July–31 August 2014,
photo by Gabriel Szabo/Guzelian

Biographies

Frank Bock
works across a number of areas, as artist curator, lecturer and therapist. He is responsible for the *Crossing Borders* series of talks, and leads on the *WHAT* festival and *Groundswell*, as well as being an artistic contributor to the overall programming at Independent Dance.

Andrew Bonacina
is chief curator at The Hepworth Wakefield. As the former curator of International Project Space in Birmingham, he commissioned solo projects and exhibitions with artists including Juliette Blightman, Andrea Büttner, Laure Prouvost and Redmond Entwistle, among others. He has realised a number of independent UK projects, including a major collaborative exhibition with Charles Atlas, Mika Tajima and New Humans at South London Gallery. He has held previous curatorial positions at Chisenhale Gallery and Frieze Foundation.

Katye Coe
is a dance artist based in the UK. She has practised nationally and internationally as a performer, curator, choreographer and teacher since 1994. She is a Senior Lecturer in Dance at Coventry University. She is the founding director of Decoda. Her practice reaches across forms and communities, informed by the belief that thinking happens differently when located in dancing or moving. Improvisation is a core aspect of her work, as is collaboration.

Nicola Conibere
is a London-based choreographer whose work has been shown in galleries and theatres in the UK and Europe. Her practice engages choreographic processes to explore the potentials of how bodies relate, investigating states of exchange between people, duration, place and other materials. She is particularly interested in the nature and possibilities of spectatorial exchange, and often investigates notions of theatricality, public appearance and social choreography in her work.

Siobhan Davies
is a British choreographer who founded Siobhan Davies Dance in 1988. By 2002 Davies moved away from the traditional theatre circuit and started making work for gallery spaces. Recent works have been presented at some of the most prestigious art institutions in the UK and Europe, including Lenbachhaus (Munich), Whitechapel Gallery (London) and Turner Contemporary (Margate). Davies applies choreography across a wide range of creative disciplines including visual arts and film.

Martin Hargreaves
is a writer and dramaturg. One of his main interests lies in the queer politics of dance as it moves across contexts and spaces. He was the editor of *Dance Theatre Journal* for over a decade and is a lecturer on dance history and performance art.

Joe Moran
is a choreographer, dancer and Artistic Director of Dance Art Foundation, through which his performance and curatorial work is produced. Recent commissions and touring include *Block Universe* at ICA (2015), *An Evening of Performances* at David Roberts Art Foundation (Frieze, 2014), Nottingham Contemporary (2014), *Assembly* (UK tour, 2014), *The Modulated Body* (2013) commissioned by Ordovas, and The Place Prize (2013).

Florence Peake's
practice encompasses drawing, painting, sculpture, dance and performance. Recurring ideas in Peake's work play with the exchange between interiority and exterior form. Her work has been shown nationally and internationally, including the National Portrait Gallery, BALTIC Centre for Contemporary Art, Hayward Gallery, David Roberts Art Foundation, Yorkshire Sculpture Park and Modern Art Oxford.

Yvonne Rainer
danced and choreographed from 1960 to 1975, made seven feature-length 16mm films from 1972 to 1996, and returned to choreography in 2000. She currently works with six dancers informally known as 'The Raindears'. In 2015 they will perform a new dance (*The Concept of Dust, or How do you look when there's nothing left to move?)* in New York, Como, Paris and Marseilles.

Stephanie Rosenthal
joined Hayward Gallery as Chief Curator in 2007, having previously worked at the Haus der Kunst (Munich) for more than 10 years. At Hayward Gallery she has curated the Robin Rhode exhibition *Who Saw Who* (2008), *Walking in my mind* (2009), *Move: Choreographing You* (2010) and *Art of Change: New Directions from China* (2012), among others. In 2014 Stephanie was appointed Artistic Director of the 20th edition of the Biennale of Sydney 2016.

Alex Sainsbury
programmes and curates, often in collaboration with others, at Raven Row, a not for profit gallery in Spitalfields, London, which he founded in 2009 and funds. Raven Row makes exhibitions, usually involving artists and art histories not fully explored or overlooked by London's art institutions and commercial galleries.

Matthias Sperling,
choreographer and performer, was born in Canada in 1974 and has lived and worked in London since 1997. His works include performances in theatre, gallery and museum contexts, video works, and exchanges that take place in public spaces and online. He was an Associate Artist with Dance4 (2007–2015) and is the winner of a Bonnie Bird New Choreography Award (2008).

Robbie Synge
is a choreographer based in Ross-shire, Scotland. With a foundation practice of martial arts, and initial study and work in the field of physiology, his work often considers processes and functionality of the body, both as its own system and in relation to objects or the natural or built environment.

Catherine Wood
is Senior Curator, International Art (Performance) at Tate Modern. Since beginning the Tate performance programme in 2003, she has programmed numerous performance works, including works by Mark Leckey, Joan Jonas, Guy de Cointet, Jiří Kovanda and Sturtevant, as well as co-directing the opening programme for the Tate Tanks in 2012, titled *Art in Action*. In 2014 she curated *Yvonne Rainer: Dance Works* at Raven Row. Wood is author of *Yvonne Rainer: The Mind is a Muscle* (2007) and *Performance in Contemporary Art* (Tate Publishing, due 2015).

Hugo Worthy
is the Exhibition Officer for Contemporary Art at New Walk Museum and Art Gallery in Leicester. He has commissioned dance artist Matthias Sperling to produce new work, and overseen the acquisition for the collection of a major performance work by Marvin Gaye Chetwynd.

References

20 Dancers for the XX Century, Boris Charmatz, part of Musée de la danse, Museum of Modern Art, New York, 18 October 2013

A Meeting Place with Lea Anderson, Siobhan Davies, Gauri Sharma Tripathi, Stine Nilsen, Pedro Machado, Thomas Lehmen, Boris Charmatz & Eszter Salamon, Southbank Centre, London, 6 May 2010

Amorales vs Amorales, Carlos Amorales, Part of Tate & Egg Live, Tate Modern, London, 9 May 2003

An Exercise for Two Actors and One Listener, Gerard Byrne, part of the *Tate Triennial 2006*, Tate Britain, London, 1 March–14 May 2006

A performance by Esther Ferrer, Esther Ferrer, Raven Row, London, 25 June 2011

Brain Bug, Marvin Gaye Chetwynd, Nottingham Contemporary, Nottingham, 25 January 2014–23 March 2014

Big Box Statue Action. Mark Leckey, Tate Egg & Live, Tate Britain, London, 1 February 2003

Chair Pillow, Yvonne Rainer, performed as part of *Continuous Project-Altered Daily*, Whitney Museum of American Art, New York, 31 March 1970

CLOSE ENCOUNTERS conference: The Dancer as Agent, University of Dance and Circus, Stockholm, 23–24 November 2013

Critical Dialogues lecture presentation, Joe Moran, School of Sound International Symposium 2013, Southbank Centre, London, 3–6 April 2013

Dance and Art Forum (with Joe Moran), curated by Siobhan Davies Dance, Siobhan Davies Studios, London, 25 October 2013

Dance Artist/Curator Mentorship Scheme, Siobhan Davies Dance, June 2014–May 2015

Diagonal (part of *Terrain*) (1963), Yvonne Rainer, performed as part of *Yvonne Rainer: Dance Works*, Raven Row, London, 11 July–10 August 2014

Differ and Repeat, Joe Moran, The Place, London, 16–17 June 2011

Do-Re-Me, Nicola Conibere, part of *Volumes Project*, *MIRRORCITY: London artists on fiction and reality*, Hayward Gallery, London, 14 October 2014–4 January 2015

Douglas, Robbie Synge, commissioned by Yorkshire Dance as part of *respond_*, Yorkshire Dance, Leeds, 5–6 December 2014

Effective Dance: healing procedure for a German Expressionist object, Matthias Sperling, New Walk Museum and Art Gallery, Leicester, 2 October 2014

Every Day, Niall Macdonald, Laura Aldridge, Mick Peter, Hayley Tompkins, Scott Myles & Carla Scott Fullerton, Gallery of Modern Art (GoMA), Glasgow, 22 March–1 September 2013

Expressionism: The Total Artwork, permanent collection, New Walk Museum and Art Gallery, Leicester

Flip Book, Boris Charmatz, Tate Modern, London, 27–29 September 2012

Go, Katye Coe, Bonnie Bird Theatre at Trinity Laban Conservatoire of Music and Dance, London, 11 July 2013

Good Feelings in Good Times, Roman Ondák, Tate Modern, London, 2003

Home Made Tasers, Marvin Gaye Chetwynd, New Walk Museum and Art Gallery, Leicester, 25–28 April 2015

If Tate Modern was Musée de la danse?, Boris Charmatz, part of BMW Tate Live 2015, Tate Modern, London 15–16 May 2015

In Conversation with Rosemary Butcher, part of Nottdance Festival 2015, Bohunk Institute, Nottingham, 7 March 2015

MAKE, Florence Peake, Yorkshire Sculpture Park, Yorkshire, 7 April 2012

Manual, Siobhan Davies in collaboration with Helka Kaski, commissioned by Gallery of Modern Art (GoMA), part of *Every Day* exhibition, GoMA, Glasgow, 11–16 Jun 2013

The Mind Is a Muscle, Yvonne Rainer, Anderson Theatre, New York, 15 April 1968

MIRRORCITY: London artists on fiction and reality, Hayward Gallery, London, 14 October 2014–4 January 2015

Moments. A History of Performance in 10 Acts, ZKM | Museum of Contemporary Art, Karlsruhe, 8 March–29 April 2012

Move: Choreographing You, Hayward Gallery, London, 13 October 2010–9 January 2011

My Father's Grace, Joe Moran, Wilkinson Gallery, London, 8–9 January 2008

Musée de la danse, Boris Chamatz, Museum of Modern Art, New York, 18 October–3 November 2013

Play Ground, New Walk Museum and Art Gallery, Leicester, 5 February–8 May 2011

Projection (2008), Andrea Fraser, Tate Modern, London

Refractions, Neil Callaghan & Simone Kenyon, part of *Volumes Project*, *MIRRORCITY: London artists on fiction and reality*, Hayward Gallery, London, 14 October 2014–4 January 2015

Roman Photo, Boris Chamatz Tate Modern, London, 27–29 September 2012

Shadow Spans, Claire Barclay, Whitechapel Gallery, London, 26 May 2010–2 May 2011

Swell the thickening surface of (2013), Florence Peake, part of *Volumes Project*, *MIRRORCITY: London artists on fiction and reality*, Hayward Gallery, London, 14 October 2014–4 January 2015

Table of Contents, Siobhan Davies, Andrea Buckley, Helka Kaski, Rachel Krische, Charlie Morrissey & Matthias Sperling, The Institute of Contemporary Arts (ICA), London, 8–19 January 2014

Talk: Ron Athey, Ron Athey, New Walk Museum and Art Gallery, Leicester, 28 November 2014

The Concept of Dust, or How do you look when there's nothing left to move?, Yvonne Rainer, Museum of Modern Art, New York, 9–14 June 2015

The Crowd, Dora García, performed as part of *Actions and Interruptions: UBS Openings*, Tate Modern, London, March 2007

These associations, Tino Sehgal, Tate Modern, London, 24 July–28 October 2012

The Pedestrians, Charles Atlas, Mika Tajima and New Humans, South London Gallery, London, 1–21 April 2011

The Sleeping Gypsy (1897), Henri Rousseau, Museum of Modern Art, New York

This Way, Please (1999), Roman Ondák, Gallery of Modern Art, Glasgow, purchased in 2013

Three Compressions, César Baldaccini, Tate Gallery, London, 7–8 March 1968

(to) constantly vent (2013), Katye Coe, part of *Volumes Project*, *MIRRORCITY: London artists on fiction and reality*, Hayward Gallery, London, 14 October 2014–4 January 2015

(To constantly) Vent, Katye Coe, performed as part of *what_now 2013* festival, Siobhan Davies Studios, London, 5–7 April 2013

To hand (2011), Siobhan Davies in collaboration with Matthias Sperling, performed within *Body & Void: Echoes of Moore in Contemporary Art*, The Henry Moore Foundation, Perry Green, 17 May–20 September 2014

To hand, Siobhan Davies in collaboration with Matthias Sperling, performed within Claire Barclay's *Shadow Spans* installation, Whitechapel Gallery, London, 2–20 March 2011

Trio A (1966), Yvonne Rainer, performed as part of *Yvonne Rainer: Dance Works*, Raven Row, London, 11 July–10 August 2014

Trio A, Yvonne Rainer, Judson Church, New York, 10 January 1966

Twilight Epiphany skyspace, James Turrell, Suzanne Deal Booth Centennial Pavilion, Houston

Volumes Project, conceived by Frank Bock, Nicola Conibere & Martin Hargreaves, part of *MIRRORCITY: London artists on fiction and reality*, Hayward Gallery, London, 14 October 2014–4 January 2015

what_now 2013 festival, presented by Independent Dance in association with Siobhan Davies Dance, Siobhan Davies Studios, London, 5–7 April 2013

Where we are not, Katye Coe & Charlie Morrissey, Michaelis Theatre in University of Roehampton, London, 17 January 2013

Yvonne Rainer: Dance Works, Raven Row, London, 11 July–10 August 2014

YARD, Allan Kaprow, Martha Jackson Gallery, New York, 25 May–23 June 1961

YARD 1961/2014, Allan Kaprow, The Calder at The Hepworth Wakefield, Wakefield , 4 July–31 August 2014

Yvonne Rainer: The Mind is a Muscle, Catherine Wood, Afterall Books, MIT Press, 2007

Credits & Thanks

Published and distributed
by Siobhan Davies Dance

Siobhan Davies Studios
85 St George's Road
London, SE1 6ER, UK

www.siobhandavies.com
www.sarawookey.com

Designed by
THREAD
threaddesign.co.uk

Typeset in Amsi Pro

Printed and bound by
GRAFOS, Barcelona
on Tauro Offset and Gloss Art

Printed in 2015
ISBN 978-0-9927974-1-6

With thanks to:

The 15 curators, dance artists
and directors who contributed
to this publication.

The team at Siobhan Davies Dance

Sze-Wei Chan, Transcription Assistant

The Esmée Fairbairn
Foundationfor supporting
the Siobhan Davies Dance
Dance Artist/Curator
Mentorship Scheme.